Memoirs of a Blazing Heart

He asked, "At what point does one start writing a book?" I told him you start when you feel the need to. There are no rules to bleeding.

Memoirs of a Blazing Heart

An extraordinary account
of an ordinary life

Claire Marie Leiter

ISBN: 1-5413-6377-9
ISBN-13: 978-1-54-136377-9

For those who have walked with me, you have allowed me to fill these pages with love and gratitude. It is you that moved me—this—to be.

Contents

Preface

The evening of my nineteenth birthday, after I had blown out all my candles (to my dismay all of them, reminding me that I didn't have any boyfriends) and counted all my cash, I opened my laptop as I laid in bed and started a new document. The title came to me like a secret I had held onto for so long and its contents spilled from the overwhelming experience of that day. I began to write *Memoirs of a Blazing Heart:*

> "Make a wish," my mom exclaimed as she leaned over the cluttered table of opened birthday greetings and greasy plates. Consumed by the flame atop the wax "19" candle on my homemade birthday cake, I burned with anticipation.
>
> For nineteen years, I quietly waited to live. Dreaming of becoming the next big thing, of being fit, of being happy, I spent nights lying in bed imagining a new me. But it was always a dream. It wasn't until nineteen I learned I no longer had to have dreams as I knew them, but a list of inevitable happenings. I no longer needed to sleep to dream. At nineteen, I realized my dreams could become a reality.
>
> I don't simply desire my dreams. I have the power to animate them.

Years later, I reflected upon that moment of emancipation from the ordinary. I freed myself from the blanket of adult reality, realizing I pulled it over my own eyes and I could just as easily pull it back down. And so, my dreams list amounted to courageous endeavors I once could only have imagined. But it wasn't just bouts of dreams or boldness for living that brightly colored my years.

Through the recounting of my experiences in words, I began to see my life as a story, and every person, a character. And just as a heroine of a novel finds strength and wisdom from the challenges and triumphs of her opportunities and relationships, so have I. For even the lesser of moments or slight of conversations became grand in the making of my story. And so, I continue to live like the heroine of my life's story; I continue to write like the author of it, lending every chapter to its Creator; I continue to believe that all things are possible; I continue to animate my dreams.

Yet I recognize that none of this was or is or will be possible without the Sustainer of all things. For, in the end, my story is not about me. My story is about what is possible for us—the ones who are seeking something greater in life than what is before us or behind us, but rather inside us. My story is just one example of a life in pursuit of entering the interior temple and knowing its relation to others, to God, and to oneself in the midst of this earthly grind.

Of course, it's a lot more fun than it sounds.

And perhaps, a lot less noble than it sounds.

In any case, my dreams list continues to grow and be cut down by the realization of them. In between that, my story keeps unfolding by the changing course of characters. In between that, I continue to see life more clearly, and more beautifully than I had some-years ago. So, I persist in this momentous trial, faithfully recording the road map of my journey with the surmise that it might one day be picked up—chosen— amongst the plenty of others on the deep shelves to see where it has led another, to see its crinkles and smudges, and to see its treasure: a common and so rare account of a young woman's search for sainthood.

Introduction

Let me explain. This is not an account of an incredible life, though don't let that stop you from seeing it as such. For I see its beauty—the formation by intricacies, the lessons by characters, and their summation that has crafted a worldview and a soul. When drawn out, stretched, the days of this soul may not be sold for movie rights—they may be buried with my bones—but they are one thread, among yours, that form humanity's cloth and they comprise the course by which I seek holiness on the road next to you.

From the characters that turn the plot inside out and outside in again, to the situations that awake butterflies and welcome punches deep into the folds of our stomachs, here is my story. Let it be as it is: moving or unavailing. For ultimately, imprinting my life onto paper is for me. It is an expression of appreciation, a tool for understanding, and a means to honor those who have contributed to the human experience on the road to heaven. And for you, who seek the story of another, we all benefit from your generous spirit. So, thank you for entering into the heart of another. May you come to recognize the value of your own story and the Lord's presence in it all.

For my story contains much of what we all experience: bruises, trophies, scarlet faces, and stretch marks. These make our stories worth telling and our lives worth living. I have lived as someone and not as someone, and sure of something, and uncertain of something. I have lived in fear, in question, in prison, and in passion. I have lived, and I have decided to tell that story.

Chapter One

Formation

THE BEGINNING

The first words I scratched in pencil into an intimidatingly empty two-hundred-page journal, when rereading them years later, puzzle me in my attempt to recollect the event or emotion that inspired such words. They echo a premonitory voice of a sixteen-year-old who could have only known of the past's heart and hope for the future one's never-changing, but if it must change, for the better. And I reread those words with immense hope in this young girl's wisdom—uninhibited by misfortune or fear, but graced with a gentle ignorance that made her heart purer than the white pages on which I would write.

> I want to risk my life to do what is right;
> I want to fight the fight in darkness for light;
> If there is any way I can change the world.

But that was all she said, then continued on as if those words were merely graffiti on a wall.

CONCEPTION

My parents thought they had planned our coming perfectly. Yet my conception took far longer than they had anticipated, leaving a gap of two years and six months between my eldest, Philip, and me. Naturally, considering the delay in conceiving me, my parents decided to start trying for their third child earlier than the one-and-a-half-year mark they used for me. But Alex was conceived almost immediately (insert dad-joke about God being eager to get rid of Alex) and we became a family of five.

I was named after my late grandfather, Clarence, whom I have admired through the collections of memories owned only by those who knew him and held closely by those who wished they had. My great-grandmother also deserves credit as my namesake because she wore the beauty of a Clara. In either case, I grew to love my name. When I see it printed before me, I feel its life. I could watch it as if it were a dramatic movie beginning and ending at the same time, an entire story in six letters.

In the years when I grew to recognize and love the sound of my name, I faintly recall many things. I remember the joy of the shopping trips to Menards with my brothers and our dad, and playing house in the door displays, the anxiety that swelled inside of me at barely ten-years-old when my dad's best friend would hit on me, the exclusivity I harbored when creating invite lists to birthday parties in elementary school, the sound of the seventeen-foot Rinker crashing against the waves of Lake Minnetonka, the excitement and pride that swelled within my navy-blue uniform sweatshirt when my parents toted McDonald's into our school cafeteria, the attempt to cover up failure by ripping my test into tiny pieces upon earning my first C in the fourth grade, the embarrassment of having to wear my winter boots around school because I forgot to bring my sneakers on a snowy winter day, the pride I enjoyed when Jenny asked me to trade jeans in the third grade because she liked mine better than hers, the hushed delight I relished when the boys put candy hearts in my desk on Valentine's Day, the times I left class to go to a piano lesson I dreaded and forged practice logs for, the time my crush used me in a science experiment and had to touch my neck to measure my heart rate, the time that same crush asked me to be his girlfriend, to which I responded, "I'm not ready for a boyfriend" (an excuse I would use over and over again), the perplexity of running into the center beam of a doorway when either side was passable, the tears I hid in a stairwell after being told by the junior high boys' basketball coach to silence my cheerleader-quality cheer during a free throw at Philip's basketball game, the excitement I harbored all summer for our church festival where I got to see my friends and flirt with the boys, the thrill of having shining moments handed to me in the eighth-grade play, the shame of being caught cheating on a spelling assignment in the sixth grade, the dawning of friendships with boys instead of running away from them, the bittersweetness of departing from my beloved elementary school classmates to move on to high school, the joy of carefree timelessness in relationships, like when I'd call my best friend after school and sit on the phone with her while we watched *Sabrina the Teenage Witch* at our respective houses, the drama of getting stung by a bee on the bum during recess, the laziness that drove me to sleep in my school uniform so I had one less thing to do before school the next day, the late nights spent hunched over the dining room table suffocating from the flood of the yellow chandelier lighting as my dad impatiently corrected my math homework, and the competitive Easter egg hunts in the backyard with my brothers.

Still, standing in the driveway of my childhood home looking inward, I could find myself channeled into the swarm that holds these memories. These pieces of our past are imprinted on our being and our becoming. For I find a trace of me, today, within them all. They are whispers. They are raindrops. They are echoes, kept within the halls of our hearts. And as an echo is an extension of its origin, so too am I. I am a different Claire today than I was with a backpack, or a nose ring, or crimped hair, or parachute pants. Though simply the same soul, a marvelously different being with a new understanding of the world at each dawning fork.

A FOOL

I wanted to know so badly. I kept asking and asking for days after being led to believe Santa wasn't real (though I don't recall how—it could have been seeing the finished puzzle I had been slowly piecing together for years or a teasing comment from a more mature classmate). I never questioned the oddity of the strange being that could fly around the world in one night until I received a doll from him that had a department store price sticker on it. The quizzical stare I gave my parents following my line of questioning led them on some roundabout tale of how Santa invoked the help of stores when things got too busy at the North Pole. But as we learn one way or another, the truth always has a way of coming out.

My parents called me into their room after days of relentless prodding on my part. I snuggled into the blankets between them and waited for what they had to say.

"So, Honey, you've been asking a lot about Santa lately," my mom began.

"Can you just tell me? Is he real or not?" I begged impatiently, hating the possibility of having been fooled. My parents paused with great sincerity.

"No. He's not real."

My heart sank through my skeleton and deep into the folds of the mattress beneath me. They had lied to me for years—worst of all, I had believed them! Shame on me. I was embarrassed for having believed in a false being. I was ashamed at my foolishness and hurt by their deception. I had believed in and hoped for something that wasn't real; I had been fooled and would be proven a fool many times again.

THE PULSE

My sneakers hit the snow-covered pavement as I climbed out of my 1992 blue Dodge Spirit and into the chill of the winter evening. The parking lot was sparse as it sat waiting for the curious, courageous teens to arrive. I grabbed the many supplies for the evening from my backseat: a heavily highlighted Bible, my new guitar, a few packages of starbursts, a prayer box, and a handful of books and binders. Overloaded and anxious, I cautiously walked across the icy parking lot to the side door of St. Raphael Church as my thoughts, desires, and hopes became a reality.

At a retreat through another Christian organization a few months prior, I had met a group of young adults who would gather in a circle, hold hands, and pray aloud for each other. Their compassion, their maturity, and their faith amazed me as I witnessed Christian leadership. I left the weekend feeling empowered to develop that leadership of thought-provoking discussion and powerful prayer within the youth at my parish. After meeting with my youth ministers a few weeks after the retreat, I received permission to form a group encouraging discussion and prayer in pursuit of a deeper faith and stronger community for greater leadership. When I got home that day, I plopped myself near the warmth of my stone fireplace with an old notebook and pen as I brainstormed a hundred different possible names for the new group: Deeper, H2Jesus, Christ Followers, the Pulse. In the margins, I jotted down twenty different mission statements, then numerous possible discussion topics. Throughout the next couple of days, my mind raced attempting to develop the perfect agenda for the evening as I kept splattering the notebook with my thoughts. As our first gathering neared, anxiety increased and doubts emerged while I scrambled to develop the perfect group.

Then came the big night: the first meeting of the Pulse. A dozen school-worn teenagers arrived that evening, unaware of what to expect. Lindsay, my co-leader, and I were in a parallel position, for we knew what was planned for the night, but not what would happen. As we congregated on the donated couches surrounding the abused, plastic-coated coffee table in the youth room, I realized there was no turning back. Fifteen mildly enthusiastic faces stared at me; I began the opening statement, which I had written and rewritten multiple times. An hour and a half later, after both awkward silences and interruptions from eager participants, the topic of abortion had been exhausted, and the "guinea pigs" left until next time.

Within that year, the Pulse had many "next times," some less successful than others. After spending two hours planning a life-size board game relating to Christian leadership, I found myself struggling to manage six boys who were fixated on a rubber chicken and overwhelmed by the idea of being virtually sheared after rolling a five in our board game of "The Shepherd and the Sheep." Another time, I watched thirteen kids stare into their fidgeting hands as I spat questions at them, attempting to initiate a conversation about the Saints.

The challenges were many, but the rewards were plentiful. Although some nights the discussion topic failed or the activity didn't connect well to the topic, I realized the Pulse's success did not lie in a single conversation or activity. Success rested in the internal transformation and perseverance of the ones who chose to take an active step in growing their faith.

From the parishioners' well-wishes for the Pulse after Mass to the excitement on a teen's face when he or she asked about next week's discussion topic, the Pulse's impact on St. Raphael Parish was evident. But in the end, I knew the Pulse was in the hands of God, and it would be led according to his will in order to strengthen its impact on our church community. I continually saw the group inspiring young teens to live and breathe their faith in the midst of the pain and beauty of the teenage life. That was beautiful. That was good. It was inspired and sustained by the Holy Spirit for however long it was needed and for whom it was needed. It came and ended a year after I left it in the hands of another, but it was purposeful and good.

Still, I wonder: Did it make a difference? And: Does that even matter? Perhaps the question is: Did it glorify God? Perhaps that is the reason to do anything and the only meaningful measurement for the undertakings of our days.

SISTERHOOD SCARE

The video was effective. Sitting in on plastic folding chairs with my church group in the middle of a gym, I listened to a nun on stage explain her journey to the consecrated life.

"Just like any young woman I spent time planning my wedding, dreaming of my husband, desiring children. But God had a different plan for me..." said the woman dressed in her traditional habit with a clean—and not surprisingly, radiant—face.

According to her story, she was normal but still desired that abnormal life. She was so joyful but had once been so sure of pursuing a different life—the normal one, the one most of us long for with a spouse, kids, a house, and happiness. I had no excuse to say that she wasn't like me, that she didn't know what kinds of desires were in my heart. There was no hiding from the possibility that God might be calling me too. The idea overwhelmed me despite my attempt to avoid its influence.

On my way home, sitting in the passenger's seat next to my youth minister, Bob, I brought up the message of the disappointingly effective video. As we discussed the sisterhood, I wrestled with the idea, and it was a weight class above me—I had no chance. Anxiety increased as everything I dreamed and had planned on was no longer a fixed course for me. The fear was so great, and I could not outrun it, though I tried. That night, I laced up my sneakers, hopped on the treadmill in our basement among boxes of old photographs that once showed such promise of what I could be—and junk that collectively expressed how cluttered my head was. And I began to run. I remember racing against the thoughts running through my head. The tears streamed just as fast from my eyes as my distress became anger. I ran, and I ran. I ran until I could no longer feel anything and collapsed next to the machine.

What if I am called to this life—a life free from everything I have come to take comfort in, a life free from everything I have come to know?

I surrendered to the machine, but not yet to my God. I knew I was foolish but the anger was so real and consuming. So, I made peace with the fact that I didn't have to decide immediately and pushed the idea along, only to have it thrown in front of me, certainly by Him himself, time and time again.

DOUBT

I had been questioning everything I once thought I knew. I was curious about the book after spending summer afternoons watching crappy TV and buying into its promotional plugs. I asked Philip to pick up one of the TV psychic's books for me on his trip to the bookstore and slipped him a twenty-dollar bill Grandma had gifted me earlier that week. Shortly after reading her chapter on "Revelations" about God, I became paralyzed with shock. Based on her psychic work, which I thought highly of at the time, she reported that Jesus was not God, that there were a Mother and a Father God. I couldn't believe it! Yet, I did. Everything I came to stake reality in washed away in the wave of her claims. My heart remained, but it was broken. The God I knew and loved was nothing more than a bedtime story that sat on the shelves next to tales of fairies and frogs.

My world filled with darkness; the lights went out on the image of the world I had procured. I felt the betrayal of a lover. I felt loss. I didn't want the truth; I couldn't handle it. I wondered what good the truth did if it stripped me of everything I knew, everything I loved, and everything I was. Maybe ignorance made me happy, and my beliefs brought me joy. The foreign and new were unwelcome in my life.

Not once before had I doubted the Catholic faith and my personal relationship with Jesus with such consequence. For the first time, I didn't care how I lived my life. I had no purpose—if Jesus wasn't God, I had no reason to live righteously, kindly, and lovingly. I had no eternal repercussions for my actions.

After choking on this new revelation, I reached out to Bob, pleading for a Catholic response to her claims. He responded quickly and thoroughly, explaining how the Bible warns against people who claim such powers—Let no one be found among you who...is a medium or spiritist or who consults the dead. Anyone who does these things is detestable to the Lord (Deut 18:10-12). And by the grace of God, the story of humanity was retold in an instant. Light overcame darkness, and it was all still there—the beauty, the peace, and the truth.

May we search out the Truth, the Way, and the Lord in everything. St. Augustine of Hippo was right: "To find him [is] the greatest human achievement" and to lose him would be the greatest loss. Maybe it was some rendition of a tantrum, but what I came to see, tantrum or not, was that Jesus truly rules my worldview. Our relationship persuades my soul.

A Dream

Shame bled from his sorrowful eyes. The pain was contagious. From years of separation, the guilt rested heavily on his sinking shoulders as he entered the kitchen, insecurely bracing the wall for assistance. John remained unnoticed by everyone except me; they continued with their ordinary conversation. Once a receiver of his great love and attention, I welcomed this stranger into our home with a joyous smile and an embrace that suffocated his words and mine. I struggled to understand

red about his return as my arms remained tightly around
rbed his angst.

te with this remaining impression of his presence. I prayed
re dream but rather a premonition of a reunion with my
uncle j.. Over ten years prior, the Thanksgiving celebration of my
grandma Ione, my uncle John, and his wife Xin Xin, ended in warfare. John and Xin Xin took my grandma to a Chinese restaurant, against the liking of Grams who did so to please her foreign daughter-in-law who was new to the exotic cuisine that is the heart of Thanksgiving. After a less than traditional Thanksgiving meal, the couple took home the apple pie Ione baked for desert and, without her knowing, the couple took the pie to Grandma's sister's, Margret's, to celebrate the traditional Thanksgiving meal that only my grandmother deserved. When Grandma confronted John about how he hurt her, Xin Xin seized the phone conversation and showered my grandma with shame. Xin Xin attacked her making claims that could've easily have been showcased on Jerry Springer or Maury. My grandma was bewildered as the years of her devotion to her youngest drifted away in the wave of Xin Xin's words.

But John was no good swimmer and floated away with those words too, never speaking to his mother again. Grandma tried for many years to employ her unconditional love, but they never wanted any of it. My dad reconciled his brother's choice, allowing John the free will to make his own decisions, often repeating on familial battlegrounds such as this one that, "You can't pick your family." We are given a family that can be beautiful, messy, and broken; some of us have all of humanity's characters under one roof. We cannot control its members; we can only love them and pray for them—because if not us, then who?

A THING ABOUT LOVE

I learned a truth about love—one that sustains or terminates relationships, builds or destroys marriages. Love is a choice. Forget the feeling in the pit of your stomach. Forget the pounding heart. Love is an intentional decision.

My friend Catherine told me about her older sister's arrival into family life. At a college graduation party, her sister, Annie, met a man from another local college. Their new acquaintance did not change Annie, but he felt otherwise. After meeting Annie that day, he knew he was going to marry her. For years, he pursued her while she continually pushed him aside. After getting to know him better through their frequent interactions, Annie understood him to be an exceptional, loyal, hardworking man who would make an excellent husband and father. It was then she made the conscious decision to love him and accept him in marriage. Years later, she was happier than ever.

For a girl who dreams of her fairytale love story and beautiful marriage, realizing that love is a choice encourages me. I have seen how love can be so real and then so absent within a matter of months or years. Our culture would excuse this falling-out as normal—which it is perhaps—but as Christians, we don't believe that it is a reason to walk away; it is a call to love more deeply, to pour out ourselves in acts of love when it is hardest for us to do so.

Sure, perhaps Annie's story isn't the romantic story I long to tell my grandkids about, but it is a reminder of the choice we will always have. When feelings fade and circumstances grow dim, we are to carry the light of love in action and in word. We are to choose love. For when love is planted, it grows.

HOW HE WORKS

Sitting at the kitchen counter where all good discourse begins, a friend of mine explained her belief in reincarnation. She had a dream that she and her brother were in an earlier time marked by long dresses and open prairies. They were brother and sister, running from something dangerous. She cried out to him and swore that she would always find him, no matter what happened. The dream seemed more familiar than a passing hallucination; it bore the same tones and emotion of a memory. The possibility that it was truly a memory could be affirmed by the tales of others scribed in the books that accented her bookshelf. To her, and a third of the world, the idea was sensible. If we could have one life, why couldn't we have two? I asked myself that same question.

And as usual, when faced with contradicting beliefs, I panicked—what if what I thought to be true was wrong? I hated thinking that way. I was not strong enough to accept another person's belief without beginning to doubt my own.

During my evening prayers following that conversation, the Lord remained faithful to his beloved. During times of crisis, I have relied on Bible Roulette, where I would open a random page in the Bible and let the Lord speak to me, trusting that it was what he wanted to say most. The message that night was from Ephesians 4:3, "...Let peace hold you together." Then I turned to the daily prayer in the Magnificat Magazine and the prayers, too, encouraged peace. And on the next page, the saint of the day, Leo the Great, was quoted saying, "Whatever is forced on you contrary to the Christian faith, whatever is presented to you contrary to the commandments of God, it comes from the deceptions of the one who tries with many wiles to divert you from eternal life."

He spoke so loudly! The Lord's ways are amazing. These consolations are too sweet to accept without shame of my need for them. My heart cannot contain his, and still he pours himself into me, filling me with his word. I can only compare it to magic, and still, magic isn't even real. But he is, and he speaks! Praise to the Lord who listens to our cries.

YOUR DWELLING PLACE

The tall and thin full-time priest, part-time professor, assigned us a dry read: The Rule of St. Benedict, which I probably ended up skimming. Still, in my hurried manner of completing assignments, one statement slowed me down: Let Christ be adored in them as also he is received.

What a beautiful way to view the human person—"How lovely is your dwelling place, Lord, Almighty" (Psalm 84:1). Christ, you reign in our bodies and in our hearts. You are in my neighbor and in me. If I do truly love you as I propose, may my every interaction, my every word and deed, be a testament to my love and admiration for you.

But I struggle, I struggle with practicing love and patience with those who annoy or are rude or inconsiderate of my time and energy.

Sure, I might not treat them disrespectfully, but when I turn away, what words run through my head or are uttered under my breath? Not only must I ask myself what Jesus would do, but perhaps more importantly—what would I do to Jesus? Would I curse at him or treat him disrespectfully? Never—yet I have. For what I did to the least of his people, I did to him (Matthew 25:40).

Praise to you, Jesus, for wanting to dwell within me and my brothers and sisters. Glory to you, Lord, who pours love continually, faithfully, and whole-heartedly into me, a sinner who turns from you. Praise be to you. May I adore you in them as also you are received.

QUITTING

After three rounds of losing, he left the Healthy Snack Walk and sat down at a table across the room. Having watched this hopeful eight-year-old step intentionally on each number taped to the floor of the church cafeteria, I rooted for his success. Our mission that day was to motivate the kids of this parish in the south-side of Chicago to choose healthy snacks as opposed to the malnourished ones for which they tended to opt, but I sensed a more valuable lesson at play in this spoiled version of Cake Walk.

I followed the boy over to his table and asked him why he chose to sit out. He was discouraged from continually losing—almost every child had won except him. I told him something that I'm sure I was told when I was his age: if something doesn't go your way or you're not getting what you want, you can't give up because that only ensures failure. The only chance he had at winning the game was to play the game.

He reluctantly rose from his quitter's seat and joined the game. To our dismay, it was the last round; only one granola bar remained. I didn't know this boy's story or his future, but I knew that if he lost this insignificant game, it might have significant repercussions on his perseverance, and he will surely have more to lose than a granola bar. I hoped that his hope was not in vain.

As I asked the Lord to deliver for this child, the first number was drawn and it was not his—it was not anyone's. I cheered the boy on who almost took a step off his number. By the grace of God, the next number drawn was his; he won! The surprise on my face probably matched his.

He was young, and I was probably reading too much into things, but I rejoiced in this marvelous lesson for a boy who got his granola bar but who would one day probably want bigger things, and those bigger things will be harder to get. I pray he remembers to stay in the game; that's the only way to win it.

THE WHY BEHIND THE WHAT

Whenever someone asks what I am most proud of—usually when I'm taking a self-guided tour through a list of inspiring questions or researching how to build rapport with people—I cringe at the honesty of my embarrassing cliché response.

My homeroom teacher, the beloved Stockmama, choir director and best-friend-crush of every musically inclined student, informed me above the sound of the unmanageable energy of pop-choir students that I was to head to the principal's office with Rose, a friend at the time. My mind began racing, scanning my activities of the past week to prepare myself for the consequences of any mistakes I could have made or wrong-doing I did.

Moments later, I sat down hesitantly next to Rose, and another girl, Mary, with whom, in a graduating class of two-hundred students, I was acquainted. We faced Principal Sanders in the cramped office waiting for her announcement.

"Congratulations, you three are your class's Valedictorians," she said with enthusiasm. *Wait—what.* She continued, "Since no one in your class earned a straight 4.0, you three all came in with the highest grade-point-average at 3.99!" My heart jumped recalling the lost dream.

Having left junior high for the big leagues of high school at Benilde-St. Margaret's, I was foolishly under the impression that an A+, A, and A- were all a fine variation of an A. So, I rejoiced at the sight of that letter repeated throughout my report cards in middle school, no matter which symbol succeeded it. And when an A- appeared among the other As on my first semester grades, I and my candy-jar-turned-dream-jar were content. But as any valedictorian should know, they're not the same, and my dream was crushed under the weight of ignorance. So, I took that slip of paper out of the dream jar and crumpled it before handing it over to the trash where dreams go to die.

Four years and countless late nights later, to my surprise, my dream resurrected. Yet, my leaping heart landed even lower than it rested moments earlier as I sat with these two girls who endured some of the most rigorous classes offered, yet I was not among them. Sure, I was no stranger to AP courses, multiple extracurricular activities, and hundreds of volunteer hours, but they didn't know that. I felt unworthy with the lack of a proper comparison, anticipating how my mere grade-point-average would not properly qualify me in the minds of others.

I rejoiced privately nonetheless. For four years, I thought my chance was lost to a substandard Health Class project. But I continued on, internally motivated, wanting to do my best. I chose classes that I was interested in, and spent any extra time that choice might have provided me (though I doubt it was much) starting a small group at church, writing and performing music, volunteering, and participating in extracurriculars throughout the school year. My years were not plagued by ease and comfort; they were gritty, studious, and full. I worked hard for myself; I thought I had already lost the title of Valedictorian. To me, that was significant. That was telling in this journey to the principal's office.

After Principal Sanders ended her congratulations, we, Valedictorians, parted ways and continued with our day at school. I sat on this information that put me in both the king's throne and the joker's chair, not knowing if it was appropriate to announce this news to anyone but my parents. I was certainly ecstatic to tell them, my cheerleaders, about this fantastic turn of events. I couldn't even wait to get in the door, and stood on the stoop as the two of them squished onto the threshold with the glass door swung open awaiting the news I had told them to anticipate via text earlier. "I'm Valedictorian!" I divulged with equal surprise to my audience. Their enthusiasm strengthened mine as we embraced and exchanged words of delight.

That feeling didn't last very long. Days later I found myself in Principal Sanders' office again, this time asking her if any of my predecessors have ever stepped down from their titles. I was being tormented by a fellow Valedictorian's gossip which highlighted her discontent in my "lack of qualifications," reflecting my own concerns. Her words—that I didn't take any hard classes, that I didn't do as much as her outside of school, that I did not deserve to stand next to her at graduation—ate away at the little confidence I had bearing this honor. Yet, she forced me to find reasons to keep it and treasure it. In doing so, I realized she had no idea what she was talking about; she never tried my shoes on, she never asked to. So as Principal Sanders said, "Yes, people have stepped down because they felt they didn't deserve it," without sympathy for the girl who was being told she wasn't worthy of something that by today's standards informed her she was, I decided I was not going to do that. I would not relinquish this title. Perhaps, to others, that decision was foolish. Perhaps I should have walked away and left that stage a little less crowded. But that stage was the best part about the honor—having the opportunity to address my entire class. I took that opportunity seriously, and, with that being the primary responsibility of this honor, I accepted the opportunity, trusting that there was no compelling reason that my equal GPA should not prevent me from speaking at graduation. Otherwise, the meaning of Valedictorian would be lost. Though I was still bothered by the words that do hurt more than sticks and stones, I decided not to listen. I would let critics kick at stone walls.

Weeks later, I approached that podium and told them about the beach:

> Many events in our lives allude to growing up. These may include our first training-wheel-free bicycle, sitting at the "grown-up table" for Thanksgiving, or senior privileges. For me, included in this list was the day my dad removed our beloved sandbox from our backyard.
>
> I like to think of our childhood as our sandbox days, and these days have been fun; but after a while, we've explored it all, we've been safely kept within its boundaries, and we've grown tired of its limitations. Today my friends, we have the opportunity to visit the beach (no permission slip required). This beach opens us to greater experiences and

exploration, wider visions and understanding, and a lot more sand to play in. We might get sunburned, sand in our eyes, possibly dehydrated. But, we're ready. For the foundation that Benilde-St. Margaret's laid prepares us for the larger sphere of life and living. I suppose you could say BSM has applied our sunscreen. But I believe our experience here is more than exterior preparation. We've learned how to build sandcastles, how to collect seashells. We've become adults. This doesn't mean we have to grow up nor should we grow up, because, after all, the beach is like one big sandbox invoking us to enjoy its warmth and beauty as we dream under the midday sun.

You may be wondering what we will do there. That's up to you. Just follow God and your dreams, and I'm sure you'll find something worthwhile. So, close your eyes and recall your dreams. In elementary school, they may have been to become a firefighter, a princess, or Batman; in high school, you may have dreamt to make Varsity, be admitted to your top college or university, or become a vampire. But today, as we evoke the memories of high school and all that came before it, let us awaken our dreams that moved us to where we are today and let them never sleep again. God wants to take us to the beach; let's follow and make the most out of it.

No, I can't recall a standing ovation or fan-mail about how my address changed people's lives, but I stepped back from the podium, the sheen of Valedictorian washed from my robe, never to be recognized again, believing that it was for good. I could not stand before my class with pride, trusting many of my peers, and perhaps teachers, let the gossip devalue my presence before them, but I could submit to the opportunity, and submit, I did.

Earning Valedictorian is not my fondest accomplishment because of the title; having earned it, without aim, without due pride, and holding onto it for what good might come of it, is what I hold dearest. And still, some would call me a fool.

Unknown

I don't know what it is like to love another with the depth of great devotion. I have no feeling of deep wanting, long waiting, and heartbreaking. I have not ached in agony of one's departure or by the mere thought of separation. Days have never seemed brighter because of another; time has never stopped.

I don't know what love is capable of doing or being. I have not experienced its breath. But I pray, I pray for it to overwhelm me like the distance of the summer moon reflecting the glow of the unseen sun.

Chapter Two

Imagination

CRUSH

My first job offered me more than I gave it—I didn't know selling knives would be so formative (though I didn't know many things at the time). During my first month talking about knives face-to-face with strangers in their homes, I developed a severe crush on my manager, named Cole. I had not known men like him before. I guess I didn't really know any guys between the seasons of high school and fatherhood, and I realized I had been missing out.

I was head-over-heels for this guy. I cherished our moments together, whether it was sharing our mutual appreciation for one another, sitting unprofessionally close during a business meeting, or exchanging unwarranted smiles. *He must like me too,* I thought as his eyes glistened by the reflection of mine. His smile reminded me of a hopeless schoolboy, and I felt like his shy crush. I loved the way he looked at me, the wide, dorky smile he wore when joking around, the way he licked the corner of his lips, how he never let the kid inside of him die. I longed to get to know him better. I asked the Lord to let me do so, and he delivered. Though sometimes I think it might have been better if the Lord didn't.

ON THE ROAD

I was invited by Cole to attend "Summer Conference II" in Chicago. Thankfully the skills I developed earning this invitation helped me sell my parents on why driving to Chicago with a bunch of college kids they had never met before was a necessary business move. So with a little persuasion and an agreement to ride with my manager who they assumed to be "older and more responsible," I signed up for the event.

I arrived at the office Friday morning with a duffle bag and my positive Vector attitude—not only was I attending a business conference with my new friends but I also got to ride in Cole's new Cadillac, with Cole. Clearly, the agreement to travel with my manager was in both my parents' and my best interest. By 6:00 a.m., we sped out of the office parking lot and onto I-94 where the adventure began.

Throughout the morning Cole complained about his tiredness. Driving under exhaustion is just as dangerous as driving under the influence of alcohol, so, being a very considerate person, I offered to take the wheel for Cole.

"Cole, just let me know if you wanna switch," I casually suggested as we made eye-contact through the rearview mirror—trying to stay ambiguous as to my true intention. He looked at me dubiously without a clear indication of his response.

Twenty minutes later he took me up on my offer.

"Do you know how to drive one of these things?" He asked, still cautious of my abilities as an inexperienced eighteen-year-old. "What, like it's hard?" I responded flirtatiously.

He exited the highway at the next ramp and crossed over to the entrance ramp, stopped in the center of the lane and opened the door. Without a word exchanged, I followed suit. We ran around the car as if playing a new rendition of Chinese Fire Drill, laughing and anxiously awaiting the plan to fail. Falling into the leather seat, I grabbed the seat belt, shifted to drive and took off down the ramp. The Cadillac purred beneath me as the speedometer climbed. I commanded my copilot, Chelsea, to deejay and I adjusted the seat to find the perfect balance between height and distance. Eventually, I made peace with the Caddy and let the baby cruise through Wisconsin. *I can't wait to tell my brothers,* I thought as I considered the upgrade from our 1992 baby-blue Dodge Spirit.

I imagined many things on the drive down to Chicago: what the conference would be like, what college would be like, where Cole fit into it all. I wasn't sure yet, but every time I looked in the rearview mirror, I peeked at his slumber, wondering what he might be dreaming about too.

APPLE

"You are the apple of my eye," he said walking away from the receptionist desk only to stop and turn in the doorway with the hope of recovering from his Freudian Slip by asking,

"What does that even mean? Do you know what that means?" His playfully pursed smile made my heart flutter. He made me nervous; I played innocent fearing my surfacing smile would betray me.

He strutted back to my side without purpose and putzed around with me. I forget why I was even at the office—probably putting in five times as much work as my paycheck would claim, making phone calls or building a business plan for the next summer. We talked about this-and-that as I sat next to the man of my dreams.

Together, Cole and I dreamed about places we wanted to go, and I privately compared our dreams, joyful they aligned, hoping he would see that too (and he might have considering the email he sent me with ideas for honeymoon locations).

"When I grow up?" he reflected, repeating something I had said, "What do you mean? I think you're already grown up. You just haven't settled down yet."

Again, my heart dug into my chest as I read between the lines he painted in neon colors. I was eighteen. He was twenty-seven. I was invisible in high school, and this man was seeing me. He saw everything in me before I even knew it was there. His gaze dug into my soul and cupped the welling waters that roared ferociously at the sound of his voice. I was captivated. I was foolish.

EPIPHANY

I drove down to Chicago again at the end of that year—this time, with my dad in his minivan for the Vector Marketing Year End Banquet. I enjoyed having my dad there to show him what the big deal was with my new job. We enjoyed a nice dinner and an awards ceremony with the Maple Grove office and other offices around the region. The next morning, I attended meetings with the other sales reps while my dad had a slow morning in the hotel and lounged at the bar.

Cole asked me to take his suits home for him, so he didn't have to fly them to Puerto Vallarta on the company trip. I lovingly agreed. We took the elevator up to his room, and as we approached the door, butterflies filled my stomach as I realized it was Cole's room, where he lived the life I wanted to live with him. I entered and sat on the bed awkwardly as I waited for him to gather his garments. We made light conversation as I tried my hardest not to think about how he slept beneath the sheets I sat on. Without any real boundaries being crossed, we came back downstairs to meet my dad in the bar. For the next thirty minutes, they stood there talking about guy stuff—Cole in his fitted suit, and I in my professional blue dress as if we were at the bar during our engagement party.

The feeling was surreal. I stood off behind them, not capable of participating in car-talk or the '80s. I watched their interaction carefully. Both seemingly enjoyed one another; it was comfortable and normal. In great anticipation, I smiled with hope for the real day. The man who loved, adored, and valued me laughed with the one who first showed me my capacity to be loved, adored, and valued.

On that trip home, I packed my earbuds deep inside my ears and shuffled through my collection of love songs, imagining my life with Cole. Eight hours later I hung those precious suits on the door inside his office. As I lifted them to the hook, I caught their scent, and it drew me in. I continued to smell the aroma of his jacket, and the blood seemed to pump faster through my body. I was so sure it was all real.

BEATEN AND PULLED

Oh Lord: My heart is being beaten—pulled. My heart longs for you, to form a relationship with you. I want to feel your love, not just know about it. Yet, I also want to give it back and allow you to feel mine. For in that, our relationship can be grounded and meaningful. Your love is all I truly desire and all for which I long. You are my life. I surrender it to you.

But Lord, my love for humans is a wedge in our relationship. I rely too heavily on man's love and care for me that I fail to appreciate you who already loves me so perfectly. The feelings I have for Cole are ones I want for you alone. Please, Lord, direct me—help me to release the feelings I have fostered so I may more freely and fully love you. I will let you decide who cuts into our dance. I love you and seek you, Lord.

SURPRISES

"...She keeps you grounded," Cole suggested, filling in the gap of conversation as I rummaged through my vocabulary to accurately describe the unique beauty of my dear friend, Emily. Bashfully, she walked through the doorway and I stretched out my arm to greet her, resting it on her shoulders.

"This is Emily," I introduced with great pleasure. Cole, of course, needed no introduction as Emily was well-versed in the storyline of our relationship. She acknowledged him as she stood in her skinny thrifted jeans, nineties flannel button-up, and male work-boots. Her pixie cut complemented her grunge-hipster look although some children would question why she dressed like a boy. They didn't realize she was silently protesting just that gender stereotype. To her humor, even her most suitable company debated her sexual orientation. But that is precisely what made her company, including—and most graciously—myself, grounded.

I suspect we all get caught up in the beautiful lie of consumerism—the over promising, under delivering giant of a disappointment. When we, the disillusioned, lose the attachments we stake our well-being in, the lie surfaces as what we once treasured departs without even a goodbye. Then what is left but the beliefs that root us into the ground? But as those roots are uplifted with the realization of false truths, we become wanderers looking for something new to believe in. We no longer have anything but the company with whom we wander. And I want to wander with Emily. For she picks me out of the poor beliefs I too lightly assume and helps me roam towards the land I want to be grounded in and grow on.

In the middle of a discussion on abortion one day, I became frustrated and said,

"I don't even see a point in talking about it because we're not going to change our minds on the matter."

I had both wanted and avoided the conversation with my other-minded friend for a couple of years. Thankfully, abortion diverted the gay marriage debate.

"No, I disagree," she responded heatedly, "I think it's important to talk about what we believe because it helps me understand you better."

Knowing I was wrong, I swallowed my pride and agreed. I once held that being a bigger person meant not talking about a matter because you and your opponent had no intention of changing your opinion and thus, you avoid pointless elevated discussion. Although this is true in some situations, for those who desire the truth and appreciate people, understanding the reasons behind the other side is more important than the position itself.

That was a revelation of her compassion for people. I pray for that very compassion that astounds me. Upon return from her month-long stay in a California compound learning about sustainable vocations, she spent two hours describing in total the twenty-some people she grew to know and love. Curious about these people who came from different backgrounds, interests, and passions, I listened intently, learning more about what my friend so valued and found pleasure in than her trip itself.

We hadn't always had this depth of friendship (of which she will occasionally remind me). She wore braids and was bossy; I wore platforms and was exclusive. In those elementary school years, friendships were made easily and then molded by complications on the playground or at birthday parties. She could attest to more distinct memories from our early years, whereas my memories of us mainly begin when we moved into Dowling Dormitory freshman year of college.

The winter days were welcomed in our dorm room. Paper snowflakes hung by ribbon taped to the white-speckled ceiling. They hung at different lengths and fluttered as the suction of the opening door sent them rippling through the air. Soon enough, Emily had replaced each snowflake with a decorative paper flower to make spring feel welcome as well. Yet, the Christmas lights draped elegantly around the magazine collaged walls were invited to stay all year long.

We spent months in that room celebrating test scores, crying over breakups, and eating baby carrots. The carrots were meticulously worked off by hula-hooping, jump-roping, or Seventeen Magazine's recommended lunge workouts to the dismay of the girls a floor below us. After an intense jump-rope workout, the RA from the first floor—who later became good friends with Emily—knocked on our door. Emily, with the hula-hoop hanging on her shoulder, answered the door only to have her motives questioned by the RA. We were cleared and decided to continue.

Later that night—and every night—she walked towards the window that looked out over the students passing through the quad. The morning had crept up on us while Emily worked on her Spanish paper she had been procrastinating, and I read from Abraham Lincoln's biography. However, much of her evening was spent on Facebook or telling stories for me she would never finish as her mind wandered back to something on her computer. Having been accustomed to her inability to finish stories since the beginning of the year, I politely listened and when her thoughts moved on to other things so did I. But as she approached the window, I rolled over on my bed towards the wall. Emily turned around and began running across our dorm room. She stepped up onto my mattress and pulled herself onto the top bunk.

"Goodnight Claire, I love you." She said as she got under her covers and unplugged the Christmas lights. Rolling back into position, I responded,

"I love you, too."

"I love you more."

"...Probably."

With my sudden snarky remark that flashed through my head, she scoffed, and then giggled for the truth of the matter was, I may have been right. I do not know if I can love as great as she does.

That call to love as deep as her was a considerable challenge, especially challenging was her time abroad in Ecuador where she revealed her contempt for the Catholic Church and God in general. Writing about it now I realize we've yet to finish the conversation that became too involved over email. Instead of continuing the endless discussion of religion, we mostly discussed the botfly that was slowly growing under the skin on her thigh. Ecuador was not exempt from the exotic bugs that inhabit South America. Unfortunately, Emily was a victim of one of those.

One day in Ecuador, she came home with a bug bite. The next week, it was swollen, and she knew something wasn't right. After a few doctor visits and time for the bite to fester, she learned there was a botfly growing under her skin. The only thing she could do was wait. And she waited. She waited in bed for a week as the pain became too intense for her to function normally. Eventually, the little bugger began to pucker through the skin of her thigh while she thought of names for her new friend—seriously. She kept the botfly in a small container to bring home as a souvenir.

After her storytelling of this unusual predicament, she told me her sister, Lexi, requested me to sharpen her Cutco knives, and a week later I parked in front of the quaint, white Minneapolis home and retrieved my sharpening kit and a few extra pieces of Cutco to show Lexi if she was interested. I hurried to the steps. The door quietly opened to the sight of Lexi with her newborn, Ameena, sleeping in her arms.

"Hi, Lexi!" I excitedly whispered, "Sorry I am late!"

"It's okay. Come on in."

I began to make small talk as I followed Lexi and Ameena down the hall and to the kitchen. Making myself at home, I grabbed her knives on the counter and began scraping them against my metal sharpener. She was reluctant to begin a conversation; she looked into the living room—the sofa lined the right corner enough to view the TV in the left corner. From the corner of my eye, I noticed the rocking chair in the center of the room move. I turned quickly to see Emily jump from behind the chair. I didn't understand and began to cry in shock. Emily rounded the kitchen counter with her arms open to embrace me. Lexi was entertained by her role in the reunion. The next few minutes we stood in the kitchen as I tried to comprehend what just happened. Emily was not supposed to come home for another two weeks, and there she was before me.

She had surprised me many times before and many times to come. As we grew, so did the number of our differences. Our differences would likely strike one as off-putting in a friendship, but to me, they were surprisingly critical in developing a tried and tested perspective on the world—one I'm still working on.

ANOTHER DAY

Oh, Lord: You sustain my very being. You first thought me into being, and it is because of your constant thought of me that I rise in the morning. And I rise because you still have work to do with me and for the building of your kingdom. Therefore, there is a significant purpose in each day. There is something you still want to accomplish in me or through me. And so, I rise with the intention to know you more and in knowing you, loving you, and in loving you, seeking your will above all. Use me as you please.

MUSIC AND THE HEART

We sat in the back seat of his Cadillac per his request. I had agreed to that arrangement bashfully. He said we needed to plan for summer business, but we both knew none of that would get done on our ride to Chicago. Naturally, at the half-way point, I tired of banter and laid my head on the center consul to rest, looking outward toward the trees of the Wisconsin summer landscape whizzing past. Restlessly uncomfortable with my sleeping position, I couldn't sleep. Cole began slipping an earbud into my ear. My heart fluttered. I helped him situate the bud in my ear but didn't move further, waiting to hear what he wanted to play for me. "You Make Me Smile" by Uncle Kracker began and I wrapped myself in my ballerina fleece tie-blanket to conceal my heart that was beating violently through my chest. I felt I needed to say something, anything, and awkwardly exclaimed,

"I love this song!" without providing any recognition of the words his heart was whispering.

This is real; I'm not making this up! I thought, trying to confirm the meaning of his ambiguous flirtation throughout the past year. The sunshine beamed through the windows, and I basked in its light, still aware of my heart, pounding. I turned my head up slightly enough to watch him search for the next love song, while also concealing my awareness of what he was doing. He couldn't resist playing the next one before the last ended, and he went on to say through "Make You Smile," "I Want You to Want Me," "Whole Lotta Love," and "Baby Come On," everything I had heard through the whispers of his longing eyes. The car now was speeding as fast as my imagination and my lungs couldn't keep up.

My ballerina blanket could have told the rest of the story. I was too young to see how this would unfold. I was too naive to grab the back of his head and kiss him right then and there. So, in fear and question and doubt, I let my heart take its cool-down run, and I continued to lay there, paralyzed by possibility.

CAPTURED

He had captured my heart and had withdrawn me from the sight of every color but that of his own skin and hair and eyes. I could not breathe without his scent nearby or hear without a call from him. Every piece of me was attracted to him, every move sustained by knowing he was on this same planet. The fruitfulness of the hours of my day was determined by the contact I lacked or had with him. From my rising to my end, I was hopeless; he was that for which I longed.

MIRANDA'S GIFT

He strutted out of the room, as he usually did with swagger and the confidence of a lion, toward the pop machine yelling,

"Can I get you a Diet Coke?"

To the walls, I replied, "No, thanks!"

Miranda, the new trainee waiting for her ride, turned to me with a grin saying, "Somebody's got a crush."

Surprised by her remark, I simply smiled and lowered my head in embarrassment. I quickly realized she could've been talking about me, so I sought clarification,

"Wait, who? Me or him?"

"Him," she replied.

Stunned by her recognition of what I had been trying to tell my friends for the past year, I didn't want her to stop.

"What do you mean? How can you tell?"

Certain, she said, "The twinkle in his eye, the jump in his step. How can you not tell?"

He returned to the room with a Diet Coke for me.

"So what do you want?" He asked standing inside my comfort zone.

"Nothing," I admitted despite having spent my day covering for him.

Earlier that morning, Cole planned on driving Nik to the office to run the Saturday morning sales workshop and training for new representatives. Cole, not surprisingly, failed to wake up on time to pick up Nik. Knowing I lived close to the office, Nik called me in for support, and being the great assistant I was, I agreed to cover.

It was what it was. To my surprise, I was not angry or revengeful towards Cole's mistake, although I would consider him forever in debt for this and many other occasions, I was just doing my job.

"Are you hungry?" He insisted.

"Yeah." I wasn't.

"Wanna grab some food at MadJacks?"

Of course I wanted to have dinner with him, but obviously, I didn't want him to know that, so I agreed with apprehension.

"Would you like some dessert?" The waitress asked, clearing our table.

"No, I think we're good," I responded.

"Yeah, my boyfriend and I go through the same thing all the time—we plan on dessert and by the time we're done, decide to pass," she said.

Cole quickly interrupted her: "Yeah, we have that problem all the time!"

As she turned away, he turned to me with his mouth wide open and eyes even wider in sheer delight of his tomfoolery. I shook my head and lowered my face to conceal my amusement in this game of make-believe.

We left the restaurant, and he took me shopping.

"I feel like a little kid when I am around you," Cole said sliding across the snow laden parking lot of Nordstrom's Rack in his Nike sneakers.

We walked through the automatic doors and surveyed the large retail outlet.

"Okay, so you have a fifty-dollar limit." I looked at him with surprise. I was overwhelmed by the task ahead, hoping he wouldn't be turned off by the absurd length of time it takes me to shop. Weaving my way through the store, I lost track of Cole. Entering the towering aisle of shoes, I saw him out of the corner of my eye, and we each peaked back to check in with the other. No words were exchanged, only a flirtatious, heartfelt smile—the kind with familiarity and joy, one that I could dwell in without the remembrance of time.

When I finally got home that night, after a whirlwind of activity with Cole, my heart ached knowing his imperfections: his unreliability and boyishness that was not suitable for a relationship. And still, my heart ached for him.

SPONTANEITY

A favorite music video of hers played on the MacBook sitting on the kitchen table. I sat at its bench, messily devouring s'more cups and watched it, delighted by the freeness of the images conveyed in the video.

"I wish I were more impulsive," Emily complained slipping into the bench next to me.

"Well, then be more impulsive," I logically encouraged.

"That's the problem. I'm just not."

"Okay, well let's change that. Let's do something impulsive tonight!"

Unassured, she glanced up at the clock on the wall—10:55 p.m. "Like what?"

"I don't know. We could go toilet-papering, egg a car, get your nose pierced."

I knew I landed on a good option. Originally, the date to get that rebellious piercing was set after graduation, then tentatively rescheduled multiple times throughout Freshman year, and discussed over Facebook the next summer. Two years later, in pursuit of spontaneous activity, the time had finally arrived.

"Really?" She asked, hesitant to commit to such spontaneity.

Although not quite convinced myself, I confirmed, "Yeah, totally!" Emily blushed with excitement and stood up.

"Emily, this is perfect! You want to be more spontaneous, and you've wanted to get your nosed pierced for the past year so let's do it. I'm making you. I'll drive!"

But Emily thought she found an out to such insanity. "But it's 11:00 p.m. right now. They're probably closed."

I quickly searched the shop's hours online. "Nope, they close at 12:00 a.m. Let's go!"

Twenty minutes later, we arrived at St. Sabrina's in Uptown. Emily was still flushed and jittery. An employee who was clearly also a patron of the piercing and tattoo shop approached and asked if she could help. Surveying the glass cases of jewelry, I turned to her hesitantly,

"Yeah, we would like to get her nose pierced."

Emily looked at me for reassurance. The woman informed us appointments ended at 11:30 p.m. and we'd have to make an appointment for the following day—so much for spontaneity. Against my better judgment, I scheduled an appointment for two.

The next morning, I ran into my mom in the hallway.

"Hey Mom, how would you feel about me getting my nose pierced?"

That was my fragile way of asking her if she approved even though past conversations alluded to her disapproval of such a decision. She hesitated in responding, and I couldn't wait for her reply,

"Because I'm getting one later today."

She cringed, and her face fell as she studied my un-pierced face. "Well, you're old enough to make the decision, I just don't support it," she said relinquishing her authority.

I assured her that it would be cute. She didn't respond. So I went and sat down in that tattoo parlor's chair and let the black-haired, gauged-ear artist rub alcohol in the dip in my nose just above my nostril. The gun drew near. I closed my eyes, and they filled with water.

I realized it was a risk—moms might not be so willing to buy knives from me anymore or peers might make assumptions about me, but that was okay. I didn't want to play by a rulebook anymore. I wasn't throwing morals out the window; I was throwing caution to the wind. I think everyone thirsts to break their own mold once in a while, if only just to remind themselves that their mold is moldable.

For what our heart truly longs for is that which it already contains.

A Gift

After the examination of conscience, the Confirmation students on retreat went to Confession while I awaited my role in prayer that evening. Having nothing to do except pray, I prayed.

My love song to you, oh Lord:

I love you so much, Jesus! I love you so much my heart can hardly contain you. Please dig deeper, come closer, move in and stay forever. Kick out my pride, my jealousy, my sin. For you are the only one I want in control there. I give my life to you; I surrender all that I am. You've asked me to be here tonight for a reason, and I can't wait to meet you here. You are alive and well in this place, and soon, you will be physically present among us. You will pour your love over us and transform our hearts and minds. Please, Lord, empty me and pour every grace into me you can afford. Help me to bring you to their lips. Remove me from myself and take me away. Take me away with you so that I may rest in your presence forever. For I am yours and belong to you. If I could leave this world, how I would in a heartbeat, for you are the one I serve. I do not belong in this broken world nor is there anything here for me. I love you, Lord, and I pray for your children. They are longing for truth and love, but they seek you in such empty places because those places are deceiving. But they will never find rest unless they find you. Jesus come and dwell among us. Take away the exterior and interior distractions, take away the shame, the pain, the suffering. We are here to meet you face-to-face. Jesus, come, and rain down your love. I ask for your angels and saints to be in communion with us—singing and praising. I want to hear your beautiful angels, and I want to sing with them. Count me in your choir tonight. I love you so much, and I ask you to pour it out tonight. Let us experience you, let us feel you among us, let us see you. I love you my Jesus. Thank you for your beauty and your bride. I love your Church, and I will always protect her. Jesus, call me to vocation, call me deeper, call me to be a better disciple, friend, musician, person, and daughter. I give you praise, honor, and glory all the days of my life because you are my creator and sustainer. I praise you and give you honor. Praise be to you, my love. You're the one for me. You're the only thing I need and the only thing that I long for. Praise be to you Jesus. All my focus is on you, and all my heart is yours. I ask for the gift to go deeper in prayer with you in tongues—not necessarily during adoration for it may be a distraction but one-on-one Jesus. As you can see my thoughts are sporadic for I do not know what to say, I have so much to say so please, I ask for the ability to love you, praise you and pray in tongues. I love you, Lord, and you are all I long for. Praise be to you, Jesus. Glory to you, Jesus. Use me Lord. I love you, Jesus, glory to you, Jesus. I love you, Jesus.

With no more words, I visited him in the closet that had been converted into a small perpetual adoration chapel. When I saw him there, on the table, in the dark, beaming from the crystal lights strewn along the walls, I began to cry. Muttering words of praise, I bawled, then laughed, rocked, and lifted my arms. He overtook me. Beaming and still laughing with a smile stretched across my face as if it was too small for its place, I joined the rest of the group. In the middle of our worship, we took fifteen minutes for silent prayer and I kneeled off to the side and whispered my love to Him.

Lights shined solely on the monstrance, spilling onto the nearest adorers. In silence, we prayed; separately, but to the same tune of a gracious and loving God present before us in the Holy Eucharist. I had knelt before him many times ago, and found myself before him once again, though never hidden, now humbled and stripped before this profound mystery. His spirit danced about me to the beat of my heart. For my heart could not contain him. But oh how it desired to partake in his wonder. When my words failed to enter the dance, my soul cried out. The impulse was unfamiliar, prompting me to part my lips and provoking my tongue as my mind fell silent. With his hand still extended, I could no longer object—I took it and entered the dance. The fire flowed from my soul through my tongue, and it was Him and me, on our mountain top, dancing Spirit-with-spirit.

To my dismay, I had to return from that mountain to the life I foolishly cling to so firmly and dearly. Upon my return, my mom welcomed me home. She grabbed my shoulders, studied my face, and said,

"Claire, you're glowing!"

My eyes widened in surprise, not having noticed it myself, nor having understood its source. I shrugged, "I had a great weekend."

Three years later I was reading the story of the Ten Commandments. As we know, Moses ascended Mount Sinai, and God spoke to him, establishing a new covenant and leaving with him the Ten Commandments. When Moses descended the mountain after his conversation with God, the people were shocked, for they saw the glowing face of Moses.

I had to read that again.

Moses is described as glowing. And though it has been noted, and written, and seen, and known before, it is then that I realized that the God of Moses, who gave us the Ten Commandments, is alive in the Catholic Church! The God of the Apostles, who gave us the fire of his Holy Spirit, who made foreign languages dance on the tongue, is alive in the Catholic Church! His word is alive today in his people. Our God is alive.

Dreams

Music class in elementary school was led by the seemingly ancient Mr. Carlson, who also instructed students in piano outside of class. He wore thick square glasses and a peppered beard crowning a selection of nineties patterned ties. His classroom activities were equally entertaining, putting us into imaginary canoes that we rowed down a river. To me, a second grader, music was simplistic, uninteresting, and quite irrelevant next to learning how to read or the smell of lunch being prepared down the hall. But Mr. Carlson knew the depth and width of music and emphatically wanted to share it.

"You've got to get her into piano lessons," he explained to my mom after school one day. And so, without much hesitation, I began a lengthy piano introduction in his home decorated by Charles Schulz characters. After his retirement, I was passed along to Mrs. Bowen and naturally, performed at recitals and played for church upon demand. By sixth grade, Mrs. Bowen asked if I was going to audition for "The Play" that fall. "The Play" was the most popular fall extracurricular activity wherein most junior high students of our small school spent their Fridays, Saturdays, and Sundays in rows of folding chairs in the gym learning songs and choreography for a big show in November. So I spent my junior high falls at rehearsals learning dance numbers and taking on small roles like the Disney dwarf "Sleepy" or a Parisian dancer—these shows were a compilation of musicals stitched into a creative storyline.

By seventh grade, my voice was heard after a forced audition in front of the whole cast. Girls and boys of each grade would line up behind a microphone as one of the parents played and rewound the CD in the karaoke machine for each actor or actress. We all had to share our abilities and supposedly, mine were pretty good. I was given the lead role as Ms. Lightrail—a beautiful, shallow actress who became a victim of a scummy marketing agency named Dewey, Cheetem, and Howe. And in eighth grade, I ended my junior high career with three solos (including one with French lyrics duct-taped to my hand), an entrance on a piano platform, and a feeling that I had found my place in life—on stage.

I feared I had peaked in junior high. By ninth grade, I quickly faded into the diverse talents within a bigger school, and so, began personal creative endeavors. I picked up my dad's guitar he bought in the seventies and searched through online resources to learn simple chords. Without a big lead in a musical to work on, I began crafting songs.

I joined multiple choirs but didn't stand out much as a new addition. Luckily, my choir teacher invited me to be a pit singer for a Catholic conference in Ohio after another singer had turned down the opportunity. I gratefully agreed, not knowing what I was getting myself into. The conference lasted four days, and it had been fun and stress-free blending into the chorus. On the last day, things changed. A soprano I sang next to had been scheduled to sing a duet with Tom Booth, a Catholic composer and musician. After singing for three days, she, like many others, had strained her voice and had nearly lost it. Why I hadn't lost mine too was peculiar. As the musicians practiced her song, I hummed along to myself without awareness of her listening. Surprised, she asked,

"You know this song?"

Without understanding her angle, I replied, "Yeah?"

It was on the rehearsal CD we all received, and in God's mysterious way, I had sung that one song to my bedroom wall as it played on repeat through the speakers of my computer. The song had moved me; it was beautiful, and I carried it with me. She alerted our choir director, and they begged me to do the duet in her place. With great disbelief and hesitation, I agreed and was pushed up the stairs onto the large stage that was shaped like a boat in the middle of the Sprint Center. I turned around and stood behind the music stand, adjusted the microphone, and shook with nerves as I looked into the stands where twenty-thousand people would soon be present and attentive.

The rest of the day, in anticipation of the evening performance, I continued to shake with nerves. Every time I thought about the song I shivered, sweat, and prayed to the Holy Spirit to bring me peace so that I would do the best that was in me. Hours later, as my parents sat hundreds of miles away waiting to stream it online, I mounted the stage touting braces and a crunchy hairstyle I still regret, and I sang.

I saw how the Lord prepared me for that moment. Humbled by his goodness, I thought I knew where he was leading me. I began playing and singing in my church's youth band, performing at school events, recording to share my music on my Facebook fan page with anyone who wanted to listen, and announced the start of my first CD. My supporters welcomed my originals and invited me to play after the church band did at our annual church festival. Bob, that faithful youth minister, approached me after, and squinting with his chin raised, he said in his soft voice,

"You're going to be famous one day." I came to believe that, though I wasn't sure how. With each passing day, the belief that I could make something of my talent strengthened. I promised myself that I would never let go of my dream. I promised myself I would not let fear or doubt cloud my passion or fade my dream, especially upon entering college.

The dream continued but with less vigor. I consistently reminded myself of that very promise and continued writing songs. I believe that we are to use our talents and abilities so we can stand in front of our Lord at the end of our lives and tell him that we used everything he gave us. I wanted to do that; I wanted to give him everything, and I believed the Lord was helping me do just that.

He invited me to play for the week-long, highly acclaimed Extreme Faith Camp (EFC) the summer after my first year of college. With delight in the opportunity to continue using my gift, I agreed. Camp arrived quickly and with great thrill. As a Christian musician who loves performing, I have struggled to remove myself from the light, forgetting myself and focusing on the one who sustains me in that place. Pride easily slips in, and needs to be silenced continually. But that particular week, I found myself removed from the work; my heart was focused entirely on the Lord. When other leaders would approach me to offer a compliment or thank me for playing, it was because Christ was reaching them through our music. My heart rejoiced in how the youth met Jesus through a higher form of worship. This was certainly a grace from God; only He can turn my self-centeredness outward.

Midway through the week, Julie, the leader of our small band, and I took some time in the chapel, where the afternoon sun beat through the tips of the conifers through the glass window behind the altar. We knelt before Him. The Holy Spirit overwhelmed me with peace, and I sat on my heels, hunched over, and wept. By nothing short of a revelation, I realized that if that one week was the only reason I was given my gift, and every opportunity before that prepared me to serve him in that place, that would be enough.

For the first time, I handed myself over to Him. My dreams, my ambitions, were nothing compared to the act of love he asked of me that week. An act of love that was multiplied by his grace and touched the hearts he longed to reach. I wanted nothing more than what I was used for that week. It was enough. I surrendered my plans, my hopes and dreams, and my gift to the one who gave it to me. He filled my cup more than any stage could.

In a way, I feel that I had betrayed my younger self, the one who surely anticipated her future's change in direction. Part of me knew that dream could never last; that is why I had vowed to hold it so tightly. I thought I would be a victim of that adult sensibility that played Potential as a fool, misdirecting it towards something more stable, something more realistic. Or perhaps I knew the dream didn't belong in my grasp; it wasn't a dream meant for me.

Now, in holding the remnants of a redirected dream, I've retained a piece of power in the unpromulgated piddling of my piano or vibrations of my strings. My identity is no longer merely as a musician as it once was but supplemented by it. I still rest easily recalling that afternoon in the sunlit chapel, the Lord shining upon me, when I learned that I dreamed too small. My dream was to use my gifts in the way that I wanted, on stage, under the lights. I had not known the fullness of being under His light, having used my gifts in the way he wanted.

An End

"Christ's love," Father spoke, with his still-heavy New Yorker dialect, to the seventeen elderly faithful and me scattered throughout the seventies themed Catholic church, "overwhelmed the disappointment, failure, and pain of his brothers and sisters. He loved his people so much that he bore the cross despite their failures and sin, despite their condemnation of him."

I heard "disappointment," and returned my attention to Father.

"He's teaching us love. But that's the problem today, people do not choose love—they walk away from disappointments, failures, and pain. They decide not to endure love; they give up because it's the easy way. But that's not what love is meant to be."

As Father kept on, my mind flourished with recaps of Cole—how for the past two years, the more I came to know him, the more disappointed I was in the man I came to see. However, I kept loving him, forgiving him, seeing past the disappointment. I don't know why. I don't know how. Perhaps it was foolish, blind love, or perhaps God was up to something.

After the next three hours of reflecting, I opened my pages of thoughts and added more. Ideas kept spilling out and eventually I found my point: the purpose of my relationship with Cole was so that God could help me perfect my love. God was helping me discover what loving is and how to do it.

"Come outside with me?" Cole asked, nodding his head towards the door, "I want to talk."

It was his loneliness problem, I figured; he needed some company during a regular smoke break. Trailing behind him as usual, he meandered down the hall toward the front entrance.

"So, what's up?" I asked eager to hear him finally express his love for me. He turned his head revealing a secretive smile of anticipation. We rounded the corner in sight of the door, and he stopped. I kept walking, trying to stay off his leash. He didn't continue. Surprised, I stopped and waited for him to speak.

"I'm going to be a dad."

My heart sank; my lungs struggled for air to reply. I fell speechless. Our faces formed the same expression of shock, though surely at the realization of different things, and I threw on a smile like I thought I should.

"I don't—I—how do you feel? I mean—what do you think?" I asked, trying to surrender and mirror his feelings as to hide the blood pouring out of the bullet wound in my heart.

"I'm excited," he admitted, dragging out the words.

"Wow," I replied, still responding to the initial shot. Knowing he was cavalier in his personal life, I didn't know where to start wondering about the bearer of his fruit. "Well, do you like the mom?"

"I mean, yeah—it's Noel."

Her name fell from his lips like an unexpected hail storm, damaging every bit of property I built for Cole and me by hand. I entertained the possibility of a relationship between the two earlier in February when they went to a Wild hockey game on Valentine's Day. But if she ever came up in conversation, Cole always seemed very remote and disinterested—sure fooled me.

"We dated a bit last year," he continued, unsolicited by me, "but I broke it off in January because she was too dependent and she never challenged me. After a month and a few dates, I really missed her. Anyway, the first time we hung out was Valentine's Day and, well, I'm a dad."

Still astonished, I could only find three words, "Oh my gosh."

"Yeah."

The conversation continued, mainly fed in between drags of a cigarette, one of Cole's bad habits he was perpetually going to end. He mentioned his family's joy of having a baby in the family, Noel's purchases of child-expectancy books, and the motivation a child would bring to his professional life. Meanwhile, I stood, arms-crossed, returning his enthused smile. I had never seen him that excited. My stomach turned, trying to digest the fact that my long-time lover was no longer, that my days of joyful anticipation of his ambiguous statements was ending, that my marriage inclination at the Hilton bar was merely a facade.

Every part of me wanted to wake up from this strange nightmare, but instead I swallowed my will and questioned God's.

Now what am I supposed to believe Lord? I thought, leaving the office earlier than expected on account of a broken heart. It was Good Friday, the death of my Lord Jesus Christ, King of endless glory. At twenty-seven miles per hour, I crept down Boone Avenue toward St. Raphael Church under the influence of a shock-coma. Thankfully, I had left early enough to visit Christ in adoration, the place I often prayed about Cole and the very place I often felt affirmed in our future together.

Only a year earlier, after praying a novena to St. Therese, The Little Flower, for insight into my relationship with Cole, did I sit in that small, darkened chapel praying to my God behind the veil.

During the novena, I had a revealing conversation with Cole.

"Cole, I can't work forty-plus hours this summer at one percent commission knowing Henry's getting paid twice as much for half the work. It doesn't make sense. He doesn't deserve it." I fumed, sitting in the passenger seat of his Cadillac as he drove me back to my dorm.

"I understand, but he has more experience..." and his excuses went on.

Eventually, the discussion flittered to lighter subjects, and a settlement was made. We sat in the parking lot for an hour and talked; he expressed his fear of losing me, how I pushed him as a person, and how important I was to him. We talked about our families and he said something suggestive about putting the Cadillac's seats back. I believed everything he said, painting me a fool once again. By 1:00 a.m. our conversation was exhausted, and I stepped out of the car.

The next day, I visited my Core Team at a youth event. Walking through the main entrance, my curly haired, redhead friend Kristen greeted me.

"Claire!" She exclaimed and ran to me for a suffocating hug.

I immediately divulged the previous night's proceedings, thrilled about the time I spent with Cole and the feelings he expressed for me. For the past year, I had shared countless stories of my love-interest, all of which were not received well by Kristin: "He's so old Claire," she would say after each story rolling her eyes, renouncing any glimmer of approval. I expected her to do this once more, but instead, she shared in my excitement.

After finally getting approval from my best friend, I walked up the staircase to the upper level where Jesus waited in the Holy Spirit Chapel.

"Jesus, please guide my heart. Protect my heart, Lord. I don't know if your will is for me to love Cole. I don't know what your plans are. But Lord, if we are meant to be together, please bless us, and help me to love purely and wholly and beautifully. But if not—"

I didn't know where to go with that thought, nor did it feel like it had any other place to go because the former felt right and the latter had no place in my heart. I acknowledged a warmth and a peace at the thought of loving Cole. I thought this peace was from the Lord; I thought he willed us—Cole and me.

That next day, Cole called me from the airport. He wanted to check on matters at the office, and we chatted about his trip. At the end of the conversation, we said goodbye and then he mumbled something indiscernible.

"What?" I responded—an unusual response for me as I would typically just go with the flow of the conversation, pretending I understood.

"I love you," he repeated, sounding the words of the heart.

In the silence, I replayed his words like a song and corralled enough courage to say it back.

"Happy Mother's Day," he added.

The next day, my novena ended. My family and I went to Mass and stopped by our favorite neighborhood bar and grill for a Mother's Day meal. On our way through the door, the hostess handed my grandma and mom each a rose in honor of their big day. Then she handed one to me,

"Oh, I'm not a mom yet," I quickly asserted, handing back the rose.

"That's okay, keep it."

St. Therese had heard me and gifted me a rose and what I thought was the Lord's blessing in matters with Cole.

I returned to that very chapel in which I had prayed about him a year earlier, only this time, I sought closure. I sought closure for something that I wasn't sure had even been opened. I only dreamed of its contents, of its telling. Still, I needed to know if everything I imagined was really within those pages, and how the story could really end. My heart was thrown against our book, breaking on contact with the thing that made it so fragile.

I ran home to a different book, an unfailing book, and poured out my heart to gain clarity. After ranting about the news, I noticed my last entry:

> I do think I have finally learned the reason for this relationship: You are helping me perfect my love. I am learning what loving is and what it takes. Thank you, Jesus.

My heart stopped. This was Divine Providence. For the past two years, I had toiled over why I couldn't shake my love for Cole, what the purpose of it all was. This rollercoaster could have been one of Shakespeare's finest tragedies. And just as one ends, with the announcement of "The End," so did my lonely love affair with Cole. Noel's pregnancy was no more, for me, than a period at the end of a sentence in a dramatic tale of living.

———

It is said that a first love will always seize a piece of your heart, and this love was no different.

Chapter Three

Revelation

To My Lover

My lover, Lord, Christ, King of my heart: come, please, I beg of you to come and free me from these worldly things. My Jesus, this world has nothing for me, nor anything that can even sustain my being. It all eventually brings me death. I beg you to flood over me and immerse me in your love and goodness. I am stressed, unconfident, worried, overwhelmed, and burdened. But, Lord, my faith is in you, my lover, protector, guide, and friend. Please, Jesus, hear my cry. Come close to me so that I can smell the scent of divinity. Be near so that I may draw upon your energy. Breathe with me so that I may be in union with you. You are everything to me, and I love you more than tomorrow—more than the spring flowers love the sun, more than the child loves her mother's milk, more than a key loves its lock. For you and I, Lord, are much closer. You dwell in me. Jesus, I love you and adore you and praise you. I trust in your love, plan, and beauty. I am your humble servant, and ardent follower, come to bring you glory all the days of my life. Praise be to you, my king.

Kegan

The door opened to a small bedroom with a beer-pong table stretched diagonally across the room that was filled with too many college students. *I'm sobering up*, I thought, turning towards the door to reload. I found Peter and Kathleen talking in the kitchen rummaging through the open alcohol bottles on the counter. Looking for more, Peter opened the freezer door atop the fridge. Smash. The UV Apple shattered on the linoleum floor, and I backed away checking my leg for embedded shards of glass. Kegan entered the room with his steel-toed boots and camouflaged hat. He ordered Kyle to tell everyone to stay in the room, dismissed Kathleen to the bathroom to clean the glass from her knee, and called to Spencer to run down to the desk for a broom and vacuum. While watching Kegan strategically plan the clean-up, I asked this very cute farm-boy,

"Kegan, I like your accent. Where are you from?"

Responding in that same very sexy southern twang, "Why thank you. I'm from Prior Lake. What's your name?"

"Claire," I offered, "It's nice to meet you."

I laid back on the couch, draping my legs over the back, my head resting on the arm of the couch shoved up next to it. Kegan determinately walked toward the pong room, calling,

"Claire and I get next game!" I smirked to myself with pride.

Eventually, he asked me out on a first date, and, well, my first date ever. At the time, I lived at home to save money to open a branch office for Vector Marketing. I was planning on moving to Minot, North Dakota even though I couldn't find an office space to rent within that once-forgotten town or a place to live other than the trailer park with two twenty-something single men with guns. I had made up my mind and was trying to let my bank account catch up. When I agreed to the date, I offered to meet him someplace, but he insisted on picking me up. As an inexperienced dater, I appreciated this gesture which I later found to be considered rare in the twenty-first century, and fretted over that moment where this guy I hardly knew would stand in my doorway meeting my mom and dad. I swallowed the inevitable, and he picked me up.

He climbed out of his truck in jeans and a flannel shirt (this only later became my dream image of a man). Meanwhile, I was in casual sandals and a black dress—a contrast of selves that would become telling a month later. He took me to a new, upscale restaurant across the street from Lake Calhoun, a circular body of water south of downtown that draws any city dweller that craves summer-time activity. He looked and acted out of place, and I regrettably was the girl who ordered a salad on a first date. We went for a walk after dinner, held hands, and talked about whatever young people talk about. He was so handsome under the moonlight, his dark brown eyes cradled by his well-grown beard. I walked alongside him engaging in the activity while emotionally remaining outside of it. I had no idea what I was doing (and would later find out that I never will). But the date went well enough, and the next day I drove the thirty minutes to his place so we could go to the Twins baseball game together. He laughed at me when he learned I didn't know the song "Fishing in the Dark" as he sang along with the big screens and afterwards, he took me to the river to go fishing.

For the next two months, we had that glorious summer fling. I created a country music playlist that took me farther away from the reality of the North Face, black legging, UGG-boot-wearing campus of the University of St. Thomas and spent summer nights in his garage with new friends. Eventually, our differing directions and opposing interests played their role in keeping us from considering any relationship longer than the few months we shared. But it was a useful introduction to relationships that existed outside of my mind, and the struggle I would find myself in frequently.

Memorial Day

Perhaps that summer I had a little too much fun. After waking up at 5:00 a.m. to drive from Kegan's cabin to Monticello on Memorial Day to run three interviews, exhaustion overwhelmed me. I sat in the dark in my large office chair surfing the web. With a gap in my schedule, I decided it would be unwise to miss the opportunity for a recharge. So, at 3:45 p.m., I set my timer for thirty minutes so that I would have enough time to collect myself before applicants began to arrive for the 5:00 p.m. interview. The office chair was not suitable for a restful nap, and my floor seemed like a nice alternative. After kicking off my four-inch heels I used to heighten my respectability, I positioned myself behind my desk and quickly fell into a deep sleep.

The office layout suited the nature of my business—the entryway fit a receptionist desk and chairs for candidates, my office to the left had a large window into the receptionist area to see candidates enter, and the interview and training room straight ahead of the entrance fit the maximum number of trainees I had present at any one time, about nine. My office window became my favorite aspect as I could greet anyone who came through the door.

At 4:45 p.m. the sharpest looking applicant that had walked through my door all summer entered. I knew because I saw him through my window as I was laying on the ground just waking up. I had napped through my timer. He stared into my unnecessarily large private office as I frantically rose and fussed with my feet trying to get them back into my shoes to greet the stunned applicant. Struggling to orient myself, I grasped for the least weird or awkward excuse.

"Haha, sorry about that. It's been a long weekend. Are you here for the interview?" I asked while using my peripherals to finish slipping on my heels.

He responded hesitantly, "Yeah."

I tried to proceed with as much composure as I could muster. On the plus side, maybe he figured having a boss that took naps in her office was cool and laid back. Probably not though, he never showed to training, and I never made that mistake again.

That summer taught me the value of down time. Throughout my life, I might find myself working long hours and away from home, but there should be a near end in sight—for work is purposeful and good, but it has its place and time in our lives. The other places, the other times, can be used for glorious recreation that drives us deeper into our relationship with God and one another. Work can wait.

New Shores

The time was nearing.

My to-do list was shrinking, my packing list lengthening, and my excitement heightening. I would soon be thrown into an unknown world with a different language, strange people, and unique customs. I was going to study in Rome.

I tried not to focus on what it would be like or how I would adjust because I knew I would find out soon enough. Besides, I'd be in

Good hands. So, I concerned myself with tying up loose ends at home—seeing friends, eating family meals, doing Grandma's hair, etc. I neglected to study the Italian Coursebook and Frommer's Italian guidebook that had been sitting on my desk for the past month. For my strategy required less discipline and more spontaneity: go and get lost.

A Roman Welcome

After a long day of John Cabot University's (JCU) to-do's and not to-do's, I was acutely aware of the dangers of the new city I would call home. Much of it was common sense: don't trust everyone you meet, stay in groups, be aware of your surroundings, etc.

My first night out, I followed those precautions, then adjusted them as necessary. My new friends—or rather, most of my nine roommates—and I headed from the Drunken Ship to Mood (a "very American nightclub" as I was told, though I couldn't comment from experience). I ditched my sandals because of a serious slipping hazard from the failure of mixing dancing with drinking and lost my friends by getting pulled away by every other Italian guy.

"Follow me," he yelled into my ear, competing with the deafening American tunes.

"No, let's just stay here," I suggested, figuring his idea was a death trap.

Yet, he persisted. And I gave in, trusting my judgment to stop the situation before I couldn't get out of it. He led me out of the club, passing a line of Italians waiting to get in, and onto the sidewalk.

We walked on the cobblestone sidewalk until I could hardly see the entrance to the club:

"Let's stop here, so I know where we are."

I was trying to be responsible. We sat down on the curb and talked about our names, careers, lives, and relationships. I studied the face of this man in his late twenties who looked like an Italian version of Dr. McDreamy from *Grey's Anatomy*. As I admired his dark hair that fluttered in the motion of the evening air or his molten chocolate eyes, I hardened as this man explained his indifference to cheating, discredited marriage, and spoke of a questionable reality. He leaned in to kiss me. With little attraction left, I leaned away.

"Sorry, you have to earn it," I said, trying to playfully avoid such interaction.

Interest continued to fade, and jet-lag overwhelmed me.

Like a gentleman, he asked if I wanted a ride home. The red flag rose almost as expected.

"Are you going to kill me?" I joked—seriously.

He laughed and reassured me of his good intentions. I couldn't confidently trust him—not from what my parents said, not from what my orientation leaders said, not from what my intuition said. Yet, the predicament forced me to question those very ones who taught me to doubt strangers. I had no shoes, no friends to walk home with, no idea how to get home, and no cell phone to call in an emergency. On the other hand, I had an acquaintance who offered to give me a ride home.

"Eliphas, do you even know where John Cabot is?"

"Yeah, in Trastevere?"

"Yes!"

He at least knew where to take me, so the only thing I had to figure out within the next five minutes was if getting a ride home from Eliphas was riskier than walking home alone with no shoes or any idea of how to get there. I continued my investigation and warnings:

"Are you going to kill me?"

"Is this a trick?"

"I am not drunk. I will fight back if you try anything."

"I will kill you if you try to kill me and you will go to hell."

After I had adequately set my expectations, he relented,

"Jeez, I can get you a cab."

At this point, I figured I could trust him; if he truly wanted to try something, I didn't think he'd offer to hail a cab (something which also terrified me—taking my first cab ride in a foreign country where I didn't know the language; it was not an option).

"No, that's okay. You can give me a ride home."

We crossed the street and walked towards a row of Vespas and bikes, but he pointed to the motorcycle. I turned to him in surprise:

"I am only riding this if you have a helmet for me."

Though I knew my anti-motorcycle mom would disapprove of everything that I was doing, I figured she'd at least be grateful that I asked for a helmet.

"What, you think I don't come prepared?"

Clearly, he must have done that all the time with the ladies, but I ignored his playfulness and got on the back his bike with my helmet and a prayer.

"Do you like to go fast?" he asked over the sound of his engine.

At this point, I figured go big or go home (though I did really want to make it home). We sped off down the Roman street. Dipping down a small alley, I saw the speedometer rise in kilometers, which although meant nothing to me, kept climbing. We came to a small piazza with a fountain, he circled the fountain and exited down a different street. Although I didn't know where we started, I managed to get even more lost and had no way of telling if we were actually going home or not. He began to slow as we came to another square. *Oh, please just take me home.*

"This is...*blah, blah, blah.*"

He continued on about the history and significance of the square, but my mind kept racing, begging him just to take me home, fearful of what this would turn into. Eliphas stopped a few more times and eventually brought us back to the main road, Corso Vittorio Emanuele, which led us over the Tiber River. He stopped in the middle of the bridge.

The lights illuminated the stone-sculpted railing separating us from the ancient river that held the secrets of early society and weaved through the development of history. Eliphas pointed to the next bridge over that led up to Castel Sant'Angelo—he mentioned historical facts of the castle and the statues of angels posted along the railing. He looked back at me; I, straddling the bike, still tried to read his eyes foretelling how the night might end. The light highlighted the left side of his face; he smiled.

"So have I earned that kiss yet?" I leaned in.

We kissed on his motorcycle over the Tiber River on my first night in Rome.

My first kiss was unforgettable. Although I still fight embarrassment for waiting until I was twenty-years-old to have my first kiss, I refuse to regret having standards or waiting until the right time. For although the kiss meant nothing between Eliphas and me, this story will live me down.

Eventually, we stopped, and I urged him on home. We sped off the bridge and took a left down a well-lit, widened street. My heart pounded through my chest as I peered over Eliphas' shoulders to see the glowing center of my faith, the Vatican. We rode down Via della Conciliazione, tourist free, in the stillness of the night. The light posts guided us, and the railing stopped us at the edge of St. Peter's Square. I disembarked and stood before the majestic church, barefoot and thousands of miles away from home. But this, too, was home—Vatican City, and though I was overwhelmed by the magnitude of that quiet moment before that which speaks so loudly to the world, I still wondered if I would make it to my other home.

After a few more minutes of letting him be my tour guide, we got back on the motorcycle I was beginning to like. We rounded the church and headed up to the top of Gianicolo Hill—a place I didn't know I would soon frequent—where he showed me one of the best sights of Rome,

"This is your new home."

These collective moments were inextricable; I will never be able to distinguish, in those moments, my fear from exhilaration.

He started down the hill, weaving and breaking, and I finally recognized that we were in Trastevere. Eliphas turned left, and we passed my school and our local cafe whose patio furniture had been brought inside hours ago, and he turned down the alley. I saw the Gianicolo Residence and rejoiced. I had survived the night.

"Thank you, so much," I said and kissed him in gratitude.

Since I had yet to get a phone (and actually never did end up getting one), I made a note in my phone with his number, which I had no intention of calling, and said my adieus—or my "ciao"s. Four floors up and at the end of the hall, I walked into my safe-haven to be greeted by my one roommate who had stayed in that night, Kelly.

"Hi," she said in the annoying tone I grew to love so well, "How was your night?"

"An absolute dream and a complete miracle."

That night, my cheap Ikea bed rested the head and heart of a girl who hoped she would not wake up from this dream. She prayed with a voluminous heart,

"Thanks, Jesus, I needed that."

C'est La Vie

I didn't wake up, and all of a sudden, I was midway through the semester. The middle of the semester initiated the internal, bittersweet questions of having started a new life abroad: How can I leave? What will home be like? How am I already halfway through?

C'est la vie. Such is life.

Time drains between your fingers as you cup your hands and hold them tight with a sincere prayer of permanence. Seeing the value in the moment, you treasure its beauty and behold its significance. Yet, the moment slips away. As they all do—though some slip with more regret than others.

But know the potential for the love of all moments—that if you are alive tomorrow, the sky is still boundless and your dreams, still possible. And if you cease to awaken, that you will be in union with Love itself, the Giver of moments, the Creator of skies, and the biggest of dreamers.

A Reminder Call

I woke up to the sound of a Skype call—it was Cole.

Rolling over in bed, I accepted the call.

"Ciao," I said, waiting for the camera to reveal my long-lost friend. He appeared in the back of a limo on the way to the Cutco factory in Olean, NY.

We talked for ten minutes, hardly enough to catch-up on our months apart. He mainly wanted to announce his newfound joy in video-chatting.

"Since I have figured out how to do this I can call you anytime! I'll probably be calling you five times a day now," he taunted, my heart jumping at the thought.

He continued to talk about insignificant things and asked no questions. Too quickly he had to go and said,

"Yeah so I'll probably call you from the airport on my way back. We have a lot to talk about."

That was a typical thing for him to say when I was his assistant, but at this point, it was strangely encouraging (clearly, my broken-heart was forgetful of past events). The heart is a strange thing. Love can be maintained at great lengths despite improbabilities or illogicalities. Talking to him reminded me of all the lovely and painful times we had. We talked about his baby due within that next month. And yet, after the call, I imagined his proclamation of love for me! How unrealistically my mind wanders and my heart ponders. Yet, I have not been the sole cause of this torture; even after this news, he still spoke to me with great affection, promising,

"I will not let you leave my life."

I loved him. I believed I always would.

A Freckle in the Beautiful

I awoke one morning with a wrench in my side—or better put, glasses in my side. Pulling them out, I realized an eye-piece was missing. My glasses were broken.

Getting out of bed, I struggled to open my eyes and wondered, *Why me?* The preceding day reaffirmed the dire need for my six-year-old scratched and hairspray-blotted glasses as I woke to a puffy, red eye that failed to be relieved throughout the day by eye-cream, blotting, and ice cubes. *Why me?* I thought

But why *not* me? Why should this not happen to me above anyone else? Realizing the vulgarity of my thoughts, I checked my pulse and turned towards the terraces and cobblestones that comprised my view and wondered, *Why me?*

Bad is merely a freckle in the beautiful, I reminded myself.

Thankfully, in checking my email, student services provided me with helpful information to receive eye care which led me on an afternoon journey. I hiked down and over the Tiber River to one of the locations to which I was referred. After a twenty-five-minute walk, I found the office and climbed two stories to learn the eye-doctor had just left. Va bene. I scheduled an appointment for the next day—since I probably shouldn't have made a same-day appointment after dark with no escort.

I turned around and walked out of the building and made my way towards home with the collection of positive thoughts: *if I never had to go to the doctor I never would've seen this part of Rome, if this is the worst that happens to me I count myself lucky, and I should offer this insignificant suffering for those who are really suffering.*

Bad is merely a freckle in the beautiful. The day had nothing on me, well, until it started down pouring. I threw on my windbreaker and laughed to myself with my crooked glasses hanging off my face.

Sometimes you just can't do a thing about it. I often remind myself that everything happens for a reason. That may not be true, but it makes me feel better and gives me hope. When a day like that happens, I can't quite reason its purpose but I can embrace the challenge. Because the biggest problem I actually will ever face, is thinking that I shouldn't have problems.

In the end, my struggles amounted to nothing of another's. Therefore, because I can't always understand "Why me?" I must ask myself "Why *not* me?" and welcome the challenge as an offering for those whose struggles sustain more burden and for the One who bore the burdens of the world.

Desire

Jesus: I want to go deep, be overwhelmed and consumed by your love. For I know there's more. I have glimpsed the edges of your might and joy. I have received your blessings; I have received your love. But Lord, there's more you have for me. Empty my cup, and make it overflow.

The Return

The end of an era welcomes a new one.

Six countries had been traversed, lifelong friends had been made, and profound lessons had been learned. The three months abroad played out into a marvelous masterpiece of memories—from moments with my roommates, to field trips, elections, study sessions, crepe runs, Italian friend-making, words lost in translation, endless meals of pasta, RyanAir flights, map reading, photo-taking, and so forth.

As the countdown ensued and time drew to a close, I realized the experience would become a piece of me—instead of having to recount the endless memories and experiences, I would hold them within (although that probably wouldn't eliminate my need to return to the photos now and then). It was the best thing I had ever done.

But I didn't believe it was the best thing I'd ever do.

That past year had built up to this experience. Upon my return home, there would be no stops in my future, no certain goodbyes to be said or returns to await. Rather, the mortal endlessness and uncertainty of my future presented the leave of adolescence and the dawning of responsibility.

I didn't know many things: the dynamics of remaining and new relationships, the job I would take on, the places I would dwell, the duties, hobbies, and thoughts that would possess my time; but of one thing I did know, that my hope is in God. I knew—no matter the turmoil or joy, the calm or the storm, the sickness or health—that God is with me and he is ever faithful. Nothing is impossible to the one who believes, trusts, and asks with humility for the things he or she needs. My God is ever faithful and ever loving.

One may challenge that statement, pointing to the hurt, pain, and suffering in this world. To that, I have only a simple request: believe, trust, and hope.

In this natural world, nothing is certain or given. Many people waste heart fretting over the uncontrollable without appreciating and seizing the controllable or handing over the uncontrollable to the One whose hands have the mightiest control. I, for one, do not want to live another day without handing everything over to Him. For I know that my plans (or my lack thereof) are just as small as a grain of sand compared to the wonderful plans God has for me.

So, as much temptation as I had to worry about the ensuing month, year, or thirty years, I handed it over to the one who is qualified to handle the future, the one who knows the future, and the one who knows me better than I may ever truly know myself. And with that, I joyfully awaited my return to the home and life I loved.

Ciao

An accordion rang into my room. I opened my shutters and peered three stories down onto the cobblestone streets. Santa Clause and his musical minion played Jingle Bells while a bag hung from their side to collect tips. Casually, they strolled down the street and out of sight.

I had two and half days until my departure, and I wondered what it would be like to return home with only the memory of that moment, every moment—the ones that grew me, changed me, and opened me. The extent to which I remember the details shames the beauty of the moment. The fading memory was eclipsed with the sense of loss and the challenge persists: why does one live for the greatest of moments only to die with the passing of them? So, I decided to always choose happiness; I choose joy. Just as I found such glory in the moment, I was determined to do the same of the past, without loss but with the perception of permanence.

I will not miss this. Nay, I will love it forever, I thought. I will love the street guitar or accordion players. I will love the pizza, pasta, and omelet sandwiches. I will love the casual strolls to the Pantheon for wine night. I will love Scholars karaoke and game nights. I will love my first party bus experience. I will love my visits to the Vatican. I will love my first night in Rome. I will love my roommates and our nine-person apartment. I will love my kooky Marketing Professor. I will love late night study sessions. I will love playing Art History drinking games. I will love weekend trips to other countries. I will love SantaCon. I will love juice-box wine. I will love Peroni. I will love the study terraces overlooking Trastevere. I will love those weeknight visits to Trilusa, Gianicolo Hill, or the Gelato shop. I will love the wonderful, unique, and charming people I met. I will love seeing Mila Kunis and Ashton Kutcher on the street. I will love Halloween. I will love not having to show my ID for anything. I will love being picked up multiple times in one night by Italians. I will love the night I became a pirate. I will love the moment JCU became a community to me. I will love that one time I tried to wear heels on the cobblestone. I will love participating in Bachelor parties. I will love being stared down on the street walking to class. I will love carrying my groceries home. I will love eating pasta twice a day every day. I will love being DJ-bared. I will love dancing with the bar owner in Florence. I will love singing with the band in Dublin. I will love the seagulls crying from the Tiber River. I will love the Tiber River tents. I will love baking Nutella cookies for everyone. I will love Nutella crepes. I will love staying up all night on election day. I will love my Art History field trip and drinking with the professor. I will love giving my visiting friend a tour of Rome. I will love passing by my friends and classmates in Trastevere. I will love saying, "Ciao." I will love Taxi fare disputations. I will love my first ballet. I will love getting lost in our neighborhood. I will love decorating our common room. I will love getting the knock from the RA. I will love the miles of walking I did. I will love the casual strolls to the Vatican. I will love the Euro. I will love those moments I felt alive.

And these memories will sustain these moments.

The previous night, John Cabot University students flocked to Scholars for one last Karaoke night. And for the first time in a long time, I felt alive. It's different from checking your pulse and feeling your heartbeat. Rather it's the moment when you depart from yourself—the part of you that looks back and searches for the future—and you experience the very moment, and that alone. Your heart expands, and you feel as if you could soar. Some would also say it makes you feel infinite, and that's how I felt as four classmates stood up on the makeshift stage and sang a song that spoke to the moment of our study abroad good-living and goodbyes. And again, I will love that final hurrah.

I was not sad to leave although Italy had meant so much to me. For the greatest part was yet to come: embedding the experience into who I was and becoming more.

The Climax

I spent my last night in Rome with my best friends in the best place on earth. The experience became more than one of seeing and doing. It climaxed with a far more monumental experience—that of being.

After our last traditional dinner at Tony's, we visited the Vatican, the best gelato shop in Rome, and Gianicolo Hill for our last view of the city. But the evening wasn't about any of those things, it was about us, the people we were and the lives that we shared.

I underestimated the significance of what we built throughout that semester. They weren't just friends—they were people I lived with, studied with, traveled with, and changed with. They were people I knew I wouldn't have in my life forever but still took comfort in the time we had together. I pray I will see them again. Either way, I will always remember them and love them.

We gathered at the top of Gianicolo Hill with six bottles of champagne. Standing at the chest-high stone wall, we took in our last view of Rome with each other. The champagne bearers popped the bottles (some a little prematurely due to our lack of experience with champagne), and we commenced our final farewells. For the next three hours, we hugged, cried, laughed, hugged, laughed, cried, etc. And when 2:45 a.m. rolled around, I took my final look and began my descent back to my apartment to gather my things and head to the airport.

I didn't cry; I couldn't stop smiling. I couldn't particularly harbor excitement for home or sadness about leaving Rome. All I could do was smile because of what I had experienced.

My last night in Rome was perfect. I will remember those moments and people forever.

He's Back

My dream for Cole and I ended with the announcement of his baby girl. Thankfully, I was able to move past the loss into the summer without Cole's suffocating leash. By fall, I was free to experience life abroad without care or concern of him.

Shortly upon my return, I attended a Wild Hockey scrimmage at the Xcel Energy Center with some church friends. Having heard from Cole earlier that week that Taylor got tickets for them, I called Cole to see if he wanted to meet up. He excitedly agreed and told me where they would be sitting. Throughout the first two periods, Cole and Taylor kept texting and calling me to come up. My friends didn't care to move—mainly because Kathleen ended a fling with Taylor earlier that year and the other two didn't know the guys, so I broke away for a few minutes to pay a visit to my long-lost friends.

I found them up a level in the crowded arena filled with over-eager hockey fans and took the open seat next to Taylor to catch up with the more romantically available of the two (though my subconscious was certainly trying to make Cole jealous). Cole sent Taylor away to get us drinks. Rising quickly from his seat too, Cole took Taylor's place, moving next to me, and putting his arm around my shoulder.

"I am not going to move it until you leave," he said, his eyes penetrating mine as if there was more he was trying to say.

I wanted to revel in his affection; I wished we were sitting far away from the world that had already closed its book on us. But we couldn't flee from it, the world held onto us tightly and reminded me of his child and girlfriend at home. And so, I had no words. But, Cole never seemed to lack them and continued.

"Claire, you're one of my most favorite people. I don't want the end of our work relationship to be the end of our friendship. I see eye-to-eye with you more than anyone else, and we have the same morals."

I turned my eyes from the game that I wasn't really watching and looked upon his face, trying to reconcile his words with who I knew him to be. His lack of contact with me throughout the past nine months made those words fall without a safe place to land, so they fell back onto my heart, stirring the hope of a fool.

Oh, how convinced I was that he would marry me one day.

———

Sometimes there's no getting over because part of you believes it's not.

An Encounter

I moved back to my parents' house for the second semester of Junior year. Staying thirty minutes away from classes, and more importantly, campus life, brought its challenges which often left me alone in my room on a Friday night.

One particular evening, as I sat on my mix-matched childhood bedding playing the guitar, my phone rang.

"Jooooey!" I said with more enthusiasm than necessary for the occasion—my night had just been saved.

"Claire! What're you doin?"

"Oh, just playin the guitar."

"Come over! Brian and Brian are here!"

"Wait, which Brians?" Joe confirmed it was his Jewish friend I had a soft spot for, Goldberg, and my elementary school crush, Reynolds.

"No way. Alright, I'll be there in thirty."

On my drive to campus, I thought about what it would be like to see the boy who put candied hearts in my desk in the third grade. I don't think he ever knew I liked him too; I had never let him know. Certainly, the past ten years had grown and changed us, and through the little I heard from our mutual friends or posts on social media over the years, we were different, believed different things, and lived in different ways. So, I hoped for little but rejoiced at the opportunity to see my long-time crush that would always hold a place in my heart.

Our evening was normal by most college accounts: pre-gaming at a friend's house and moving to a house party. By the time we made it to the party, the talking fully commenced to the point of telling Reynolds about my elementary school crush on him, diary writings that I shamefully hid in my drawers, and politics. I was leaning against the doorway frame leading into the kitchen making some awkward comment when he asked,

"What if I told you I think you're cute and we should kiss?"

My wildest dreams had come true. Well, almost. Upon his offer, I quickly considered the situation: my beer breath, the house party, our level of intoxication. If I actually thought wildly enough to dream about this moment, it wouldn't have looked like this. I tried to come up with some cute excuse that both kept him from tasting my bad breath while alluding to my interest in his offer and settled for saying,

"As proud as our junior high selves would be right now, I don't kiss at the first party."

But it wasn't sufficient, and he continued giving reasons why we should and I kept lightly turning it down, suggesting another time. He had already waited years for this moment; I was confident he could hold on a little longer. I just didn't want my first kiss with Brian to be at a random party in front of our friends. Nor did I think it was appropriate considering the condition of our friendship (if one can even call that friendship if we hadn't talked in seven years).

Okay fine, I was scared. I was scared that he would think I was a bad kisser, sacred it'd be awkward, scared about the next step, or the lack thereof.

I woke up the next morning on Joey's couch in the living room, with a deep sense of regret. I don't believe in having regrets when we act in earnest—we make decisions based on what we're capable of based on what we know and what we believe at the time. We can't fault ourselves for that. Still, I felt it, and my regretfulness made me bury my head deep into the pillow that morning. Minutes later, I walked out the front door, down the icy steps with great determination to receive that same offer I was too scared to accept the night before.

An Accident

I had just left Mass on a Tuesday morning. It was going to be a great day—I was on winter break and Kathleen was coming over to have breakfast with me. A bus and I came to a four-way stop; I let the bus go first (it surely had a more important morning schedule to maintain), and

I followed it towards the main road. But it stopped and I didn't. My front bumper, grill, and headlights that my dad had recently polished were smashed under the yellow bus that then became my only view from my windshield.

A wave of shock and disbelief washed over me. I thought maybe—I thought it couldn't be real. But my right hand felt the shifter as I shifted to reverse and my right foot felt the pressure of the gas pedal and my eyes saw my crinkled hood coming out from under the bus, and my ears heard the awful scraping sound. It was real.

I wished it wasn't. I wish I lived in a universe with an undo button or the control of time to return to the moments of certainty and peace. But in this world, good people make mistakes, and those mistakes are undoable.

It wasn't undoable, so I wondered what I should do next. I followed the flow of time-important matters—I called Kathleen to cancel our plans, then called Dad as he was the car-man and often had the most flexible work schedule, then called Mom because I couldn't get ahold of Dad.

"Mom," I let out through my shock-induced lips, "I'm okay, but I just got in a car accident. I am so sorry; I called Dad; no one is hurt; I am so sorry."

I tried to announce all the important information in the least alarming way, still waiting for the opportunity to undo it all.

"Claire, it's okay, I am leaving work right now. I am on my way," my mother said efficiently and calmly as I sat still while my heart attempted to escape through my chest.

I gained the courage to step out of my vehicle as others passed and stared. Avoiding the wreckage in the front, I walked around the back of my car and up to the door of the bus. As I walked cautiously, trying to swallow my embarrassment to speak to the bus driver who would surely be annoyed, I heard a kid through the frosted window yell:

"You crazy lady!"

I can laugh about it now, but it didn't help at the time. In the following sequence of activities, I tried talking to the bus driver who disappeared among his students to confirm their safety, I prepped my insurance for the police, gave them the necessary information, and waited for a tow truck and my angel to come while still looking for the undo button.

Sitting on the curb facing my despicable car, the fortress of a bus, and the pieces of my headlights strewn mercilessly on the pavement, I couldn't help, in my moment of despair, ask God,

"Seriously? Lord, I just woke up early on my day off to celebrate the Mass with you, and this happens? Really?"

I had an expectation of God: if I lived rightly and did my best, he would take care of me. My expectation was tested, and God wasn't living up to it.

When my mom finally arrived, I sunk into the passenger seat of her van and began to bawl. After hearing of the possibility of the car being totaled, realizing the inconvenience this made for everyone, and envisioning my precious Sonata mutilated, I wept. As a mom does, mine felt my sorrow and reassured me that everything would be okay, "You'll see."

My mom was right. Kathleen still ended up coming over that day—instead of pancakes we had pizza. One of our conversation topics led me to check my bank account which revealed, despite my belief that it would contain only pennies due to my past three months abroad, I had an unexpected deposit from a student loan reimbursement and a previous job's withholdings return. I suddenly had eight hundred dollars to my name. With that, paired with Kathleen's suggestion to check out a used parts website to repair my car, I realized it would be okay.

My expectation of God was based on the limits of my human mind, not on the tenderness of the Creating Spirit. So, I questioned him in my hour of disappointment and couldn't conceive how he would use this accident to love me. But he did; God took care of me like I always believed. I don't understand how he can be so faithful to me but somehow, he is, and I never tire of it.

"Give thanks to the Lord for he is good. His mercy endures forever" (Psalm 107:1).

Happiness

Our problem is not being in awe of the world—the possibilities, the beauty, the advancements of our people and technology. Every moment we choose to see mediocrity instead of standing astonished before the wonders of our everyday lives, we fail to recognize the greatness of God, thus fail to love him, and thus fail to know our origin to which our being must strive towards.

Heartspeak

The heart grows stronger with every thought of God. Every contemplation brings Heaven closer to reality on Earth. The beauty becomes brighter; the good more readily reveals itself. The good things of this earth fail to compare to its secular counterparts of sin and evil. Oh, how wretched is the uncontemplated soul and how far is it removed from its purpose?

Lord, how I want to grow into you. I want to be closer and more united to truth. Jesus, I can't do it in the midst of this world. I can't love you like my heart is made for. Every day I struggle to turn my attention towards you. I am weak and undisciplined. I am not made for this world. How do I sustain a life of devotion outside of a convent or secluded home? Teach me, oh Lord, the way of life you desire for me. Help me filter through the messages of this world so that I may hear only yours and trust in it joyfully and faithfully. Come, oh Lord, and fill me with your light and love. I trust in you, Jesus. Praise be to you.

I want to do something that means something. That brings something to life; makes something thrive. I want to bear a heart that throbs with joy and sings an eternal song of praise. I want to bear a mind that never ceases to contemplate the love of God or see the face of God. Let the stars tell of the hidden spaces of God and the moon reflect his glory. Lord, I am your servant in all ways and in all things. When I forget to listen or submit to your call, correct me. When I disobey or misbehave, raise it to my attention and show me how I can repay you. Lord, I want to do beautiful things in your name. I do not want anything but the mere joy of doing what you will for another's sake. For Lord, there is work to be done here, not for the sake of earning reward but for reaping a harvest, producing fruit. That is the purpose of work and the fulfillment of it. The one who claims his product is not aware of the purpose of production but merely of what he can take away. No man gains happiness by doing for himself. When work is conducted in a manner of humility, joy, and heart, that is when man is acting most accordingly with his nature and will see lasting joy beyond recognition.

Lord, guide my heart. Lead it. Help me not fear emotions, intimacy, or the bond with man. Lord, I shy away from that union in discomfort and distress. Lord, that is not what you want for me, is it? Teach me how to welcome the new and take comfort in your will for me.

Lord, I fear the pursuit of money and material demands. Lord, I fear this inclination will be a lifelong struggle if I am to remain a participant of this society and world. A professor of mine mentioned the demands of his wealthy friends for more homes and cars and assets, when twenty years ago, their wildest dream was to be where they are today. Jesus, Satan has a grip as he utilizes our weaknesses and the availability of their pursuit to drag our hearts deeper into submission of this world. How can we find the peace promised to us by you, our Lord, Jesus Christ? How can we remain steadfast in true joy and peace?

Jesus, I love you. I love you more than myself. I love you with my whole heart, every part of me.

Lord, set my heart on fire. Burn away the impurities and filth that cloud me. I adore you Christ and thank you for everything you are. You alone are God, the source of all good. I praise you, Jesus.

Lord, I want to live without fear of loss, without desire for what is temporal, without the pain of emptiness. Lord, only you fill the great depths of my heart. In you I find all that satisfies. In you I am whole. Lord, make my heart pure, set it afire with love and passion for what you love. Lord make my heart be like yours, break it for what breaks yours. Come, Jesus, come. Teach me the truth of the world.

Lord Jesus, your Holy Spirit moves about me, heightening my senses, inspiring my actions, and deepening my capacity to love. Without you, love is only a hope, peace—merely a dream. I adore you Jesus, the way that you love me, the way that you time things so perfectly, the way you ardently desire my heart and my adoration. You fulfill my greatest hungers; you quiet the greatest storms. In you, I will always put my trust. I may not often understand why you do the things you do, nor do I believe I have felt the greatest tests of faith, but Lord, I will always stand by you in faith. For I believe. I believe that everything will be okay. I believe that you are the source of life and love. I believe that this life doesn't hold the capacity for our greatness and the holy ones we could be. I believe in the perfect timing of all things. I believe you are present and alive. Oh, Lord, inspire my heart to do the least and greatest of your works in perfect humility and joy. Christ, adorn me with your greatest love and mercy. Awake me to your glorious wonders here on earth. Jesus, come and fill this place with your grace.

Forever

He strutted down the row of customers waiting for their meals—his shoulders back, light reflecting off his glasses, and the smirk of pleasure I had seen a thousand times. My heart fluttered as I saw my friend again and I smiled warmly as I greeted him with a drawn out "Hi."

We embraced.

The minor words exchanged were nothing more than warmups for the conversation to come.

"Do you want to order right away?" I added as we stood just behind the line of moms with their pre-teens at Panera.

"Actually, I'm kind of feeling a bloody mary. Wanna go over to Wild Bill's?"

Always ready for a drink, I eagerly agreed. We exited Panera and crossed the main street of one of the many eating districts in town.

We sat down at the bar next to a biker couple who had been married twenty-five years. They were older but alive with the spirit of adventure and triumph from the years of their separate divorces, kids, and pasts. They asked us how long Cole and I had been dating. We both paused for what seemed like too long.

"Oh, no, we're not dating," I said matter-of-factly as if there was nothing weird about our chemistry or body language. Curious, they asked us how old we were, guessing twenty-six or twenty-seven.

"I'm twenty-nine. She's twenty-one," Cole jumped in pointing to himself and proudly joked, "I am a cradle robber!"

They laughed. But I, unknowingly broken by the past, continued harshly,

"But the really sad part is that he has a cradle at home with another woman!"

They laughed again, but Cole leaned away from me with his jaw dropped low enough to blanket his neck. My coy apologetic face quickly disappeared when I realized I finally said what I had wanted to say about his poor decision-making. Still, I shrugged playfully to evade blame of wrongfulness. The poor guy knew I was right.

The class project of mine that brought us together kept getting ignored as we caught up on his life and Vector office. Multiple times he mentioned that he told Noel he was at our friend Nik's office.

"Is that wrong?" he asked mischievously.

My argument increased in strength the more he kept asking, seemingly seeking my approval. So, we discussed relationships and marriage. I expressed my frustration with our friendship.

"What do you mean by that?" he asked.

"You don't make an effort to see me. It makes me feel like you don't care about our relationship."

He responded kindly, "I hope you know me well enough to know that's not the case."

"But actions speak louder than words, Cole, and yours do not often say that."

"Well, you need to understand that because of the situation, there are limited times and places I can meet you."

He transfigured me into the other woman. I knew he was right. Of course, he was right, and I was still trying not to see my misplaced passion. I had so greatly desired always to be perceived as his assistant manager. I wanted to remain in the excused zone for serious conversation rather than the friend that I had consequently become since quitting Vector. We both had ignored the change for too long, and he was giving up the resistance, he was admitting the reality. Meanwhile, in my foolishness, I considered everything to be impermanent, except my vision of our future together.

"But Cole, why didn't you just tell Noel you're helping me with a project? You are! Why is that such a big deal?"

"It's not but," we both held our breath, "what makes it harder is that a couple of weeks ago, she brought up the fact that you had a thing for me."

Shit. How in the world did she find that out? This is so awkward. I thought to myself trying to conjure up some dignity and something helpful to say in that moment.

"How does she know that?" I asked, hopefully as calm as I wanted it to come out.

Trying to make it less awkward, he said, "I don't know. Maybe Andrea? They talk a lot."

I doubted that. I knew the two girls were close but I never admitted to having a thing for him the one time Andrea and I talked about Cole—I knew better than that.

I remember sitting in Starbucks across the street from the hotel conference room that Andrea and I had fled from during a Division Meeting in the Vector summer we had already given up on. We talked for hours about Vector, relationships, and life. I wish I remembered how Cole was brought into the conversation. Perhaps I was feeling carefree as a soon-to-be Roman traveler; perhaps I had finally wanted to let her in on my heart. I do recall approaching my description carefully as not to subject myself to too much vulnerability. We discussed Cole's power of getting people to like him. I put the blame on him, that he said way too many forward things and alluded to way too many of his inappropriate thoughts. I tried playing the victim suggesting he got me to love him. But I clarified: not a romantic love, but a deep-rooted friendship love. It was the truth—kind of, but try explaining that to someone without them perceiving the relationship differently, even though it was exactly what she thought. I must not have successfully described the relationship. Or maybe I wasn't that good at hiding my feelings for Cole. Regardless, Noel found out, complicating my relationship with Cole even more.

Still trying to gain clarification without admitting anything, I asked,

"Wait, what exactly is she talking about anyway? Like that one time years ago when we had that conversation?"

"What conversation?" He asked.

Trying not to extrapolate too many awkward and humiliating details of my text, I clarified,

"You know, that time I asked you if you liked me..."

My super smart and experienced younger friend from church did that with a guy she liked at work. She got a clear answer from him, and I was envious of her resolve. Desperately wanting to quit questioning his every move and word and thought, I gave in and decided I needed to text him and put my suffering to bed. Little did I know it was only beginning. So I texted him:

"I hate to ask this, especially over text, but do you like me?" I threw the phone on my desk like its vulnerability was contagious and ran to the bathroom in disbelief of what I had just done. After a few minutes, I gained the courage to face my room again. By the time I walked in, I could hear my phone ringing—it was Cole. Afraid my parents would hear this humiliating conversation, I took the call downstairs and onto our front porch (which unfortunately was right beneath my parents' bedroom anyway). After a few minutes of clarifying my reasoning, Cole said,

"No," and tried to soften the blow by saying,

"well, maybe if it were another time or another place." Then he had the audacity to ask me if I liked him—not prepared for that question I did what I could and told him yes but not in the "let's get married" sense (that, of course, being a lie). I had to face him in the office the next day, but in a few days, it was water under the bridge. But evidently, some water had been rerouted.

"Yeah, I don't know. She didn't say how she heard," Cole responded.

Sure she didn't; I could hardly trust the things he said. But I wanted the conversation to end because I still had no idea how to handle it.

Somehow the conversation turned to me (only an hour after we had gotten together). At this point in my life, I was confused, lost, excited, overwhelmed, and overextended. Life was good but in certain ways too good. I had two fruitful jobs, I was taking classes at a reputable college, and I had an incredible network of family and friends—more than enough to rejoice about. Tears welled in my eyes as I described how I was feeling. He hugged me, pushed me away just far enough to see my face and caught the tear that began to roll down my face and wiped it away. My heart began destroying itself again.

After a game of Bar-go and some delightful conversation, we decided to leave. I cannot recall the conversation on our walk to our cars, but I remember snuggling into the fold of his arm as we walked. His arm extended around my back and mine around his. I felt safe and in the arms of a friend; I felt at home. We crossed the street, found our cars and hugged goodbye. As I walked away, we continued the Minnesotan goodbyes, and I turned around to finish.

"Cole, I'll love you forever," I ended.

I don't remember what he said—if he responded at all. I just smiled lovingly and got into my car.

Although we'd spoken such words before, this time felt different. As much as I replayed the afternoon over and over in my head, beating myself up over responses I should've had or things I should've said, I never regretted telling him the ultimate, unchanging truth of my heart. I didn't care if he felt the same because the joy I felt in loving him was worth any rejection or doubt on his part. I knew I'd love him forever no matter what would change. He was a central character in my development and I am forever grateful for him, every part of him, despite any character flaws I would call him out on, even *for* those character flaws. I believed I would love him forever.

The Paramount

One's perspective will measure one's life experiences. One life can be calculated with great delight or bounties of sorrow. And with each moment, great joy or deep sadness. Yet, at the end of the day, one thing remains: God is still God and still bigger than all things.

Mom called.

"Claire?" She asked between seconds of silence and searches for breath lost within tears.

Seven possible scenarios crowded my thoughts, each fighting for attention. Without her response, I hesitantly asked, "Mom, what is it?"

"It's Philip," escaped her voice with great pain. "He got another DUI this morning."

As my heart sank into my stomach, Mom mustered on in between short breaths and the suppression of tears how Philip had to stay in jail through the weekend until the bail office opened on Monday.

Without enough time to fully gather the wave of emotions that knocked me over and scattered around me, I responded levelly.

"Mom, everything's going to be okay," I reminded her, yet not as a proven echo from my childhood failures but as an objective observation. "This is not the end of the world. We'll figure this out. It's going to be okay."

Five minutes later, after more gasps for air and perplexed thoughts, I hung up the phone, got into the shower, and wept.

It was as if I stripped myself of myself and entered into the isolation, within the three tiled walls and curtain of my shower, and into that of a broken and incarcerated Philip. The empathy invaded, and the situation worsened. I imagined wanting to take everything back five times over. Oh, how he must be sick longing to do it over, longing to say, "No," longing to go back. How he must ache with hopelessness, despair, disappointment, and fear, and shame. How he must shutter at the wretchedness of the future consequences: the loss of driving privileges, the impact of work, the struggle for normalcy. How he must hate himself. And I wept in disgust.

The thing was, Philip was not merely incarcerated, he had torn himself further from hope with this misstep and poor calculation.

Thinking about him and his choice, I could not have sympathized with such agony having never filled his shoes. Yet, seeing with his eyes, being present where he was, I longed for the love of Christ. The only prayer I deemed worthy of heartspeak was for God to shower his love and mercy upon Philip—to overwhelm him with the greatest of joy and the deepest of peace. I prayed the Lord would embrace Philip not for what he did or where he was, but for simply being wanted, wanted by the God of the stars, the sun, and the sea. For that is what our hearts long for every morning we rise. Suffering lowers our defenses, allowing us to see our need for God. We can beget a new hope when we recognize who we are in our Father's eyes and that we are good, beautiful, and wanted.

Right now, in this moment, God is still God and God is bigger than all of this. Yet, we carry on as if the summation of our mother's tears or the paramount of our brother's pain surpasses the breadth of God. But no matter how we do the math, God always amounts tenfold. And to me, that is the only assurance I need.

Plans

Lord: I can't do anything about tomorrow today, nor do I need to know what I will do tomorrow, for you have plans, plans for me to prosper and harvest, plans for good. Must I have my own then? No, all I need to do is to listen to your plan, for it is good, as are you.

Tomorrow may not even come. With that in mind, I rest with great thanks for this day and my whole life, with great sorrow for my offenses, and great gladness in your promise. You are forever holy and good; you are forever God. I love you, Lord, and desire only what is in your Sacred Heart, for this life is too uncertain and unfair to make plans. I trust in you, oh Lord, Giver of Days.

A Welcomed Visit

Young hopefuls were packed back-to-back, dancing and drinking around us. One of the latest hits blared from the surrounding speakers and words between friends or new crushes were only exchanged in shouts. It was one of his visits to the cities, and I was glad to join him and the usual group for a night out. As we tended to return to one another, like moths to a flame, we found ourselves in a sea of others and somehow still alone. Brian drew smoothly towards me, and I accepted the kiss of my lifelong crush. I pulled away, laughing sweetly in disbelief.

I can't remember many details that followed except my fingers having naturally gravitated towards his on our walk home, interwoven as not to be separated. He twirled me around before him, and we carried on as if it was all normal and real. And once again, I learned I still didn't dream big enough.

The Twenties

Our twenties: the years of self-discovery. Having turned twenty-one, I was aware of my approaching adulthood and welcomed it gracefully, but not always genuinely. Lists crowded the internet advising youths to cherish their able bodies, love their family, make smart decisions— among other things adults wished they knew when they were younger.

The most common warning was that of comparison. During these shifting years, people will compare themselves to the status and happiness of others, especially those who believe status and happiness are one and the same. There will always be someone who makes more money, who has a "better" job, who is more "successful" than us. Comparison is misery. But there will always be someone who has less than us in every aspect of life. So, whom will we choose to compare ourselves to if we mistakenly decide to do so?

We do not have to do so at all. I found when I was most satisfied with myself and doing something I loved and was passionate about, I was happier for others' fortunes. I would celebrate their personal and professional victories. When we have discovered and indulged in meaningful pursuits, we stray from pitiful comparisons and lead happier lives.

However, like most things, such pursuits are easier said than done. Sometimes I could not tell which path exuded greater meaning and purpose for me—one that would deploy my greatest strengths and reach my highest aspirations. Therefore, because of my professional insecurities, I would resort to comparing myself to others who seem to have meaning and direction in their lives.

The focus needed to change. I needed to focus on what is proven to be a meaningful pursuit, which is the pursuit of our Lord. To pursue him first, above all things. No other chase is more important. And when our desires are rightly ordered, he can guide us in even those small things we must pursue, the adventures we must take, and the work we must take on. He wants to guide us; he's asking us to let him. We need only accept his fervor for us and our lives, and the fruits of our twenties will be evident.

––––––

You were born from intention, so live with intention.

The Painter

"Fantastic, and you?" My mother asked the shop clerk as he rose from his chair and peered over the counter to greet us. Seemingly surprised by her response, he delightfully replied,

"I am fantastic as well!"

"Wow, that is a beautiful dress you have," he said turning to me, and without a moment for me to express my appreciation, he continued,

"You know what? I think more women should wear dresses. They should wear them every day in the summer. Oh, and that necklace! Come here, let me look at it!" I took a step towards the gentleman; his brown eyes drew me in with no hesitation as he hopped onto the counter. I lifted the silver beaded necklace towards him,

"That is a great necklace."

"Have you heard of Target?" I asked with a genuine playfulness.

"Have I heard of Target?" He repeated.

"Yeah, I bought it while I worked there this summer," I explained.

"She interned there," my mom not humbly interjected as she joined us by the counter with her favorite notecards we had come for. As if he wasn't even listening (which later I figured he probably doesn't listen very much anyway), he commented,

"I was just saying how I think every girl should wear dresses. But not just any dress, those sundresses, the ones that tie around the neck and dip low in back—all different colors! Oh, how they got me." He motioned to the deck outside the front door. The sun highlighted the grains in the dark wood and the green leaves that moved among the branches. Men crowded the benches outside the row of shops, waiting for their wives who came for expensive clothing and decor. But this store clerk pointed towards the absence of them all, the idea of a woman.

"Girls would stand in the sun, and these sheer dresses would move about them. They'd make men go weak at the knees!" My mom set the packs of notecards next to him on the counter. He hopped off.

"I painted those you know."

"You did?!" She exclaimed, ecstatic to meet the man whose Eagle Bluff Lighthouse work adorned our living room wall. She pointed to a copy of the painting resting against a boat-turned-display-case near her feet.

"That painting hangs above our piano at home!"

"Oh, it's no big deal, but yeah, that's me, Fred." The business card he handed her established some authenticity for the stories that were to follow. He casually headed towards the other side of the shop,

"Let me give you a tour." For the next five minutes, Fred weaved through the artwork scattered throughout the floor pointing to shorelines, lighthouses, barns, and other common yet exquisite sites he recreated for tourists who wished to take a piece of Door County home with them. He stopped in the corner near the fading sunset over Ephraim Bay to prattle about his achievements and many talents.

"Oh, I have lived a very good life," he said with the smile of a little boy pleased with his Christmas gifts. He stood firmly with his legs apart; his hands told stories meant for fiction novels.

"You've just got to go get life. I flip million-dollar homes in two days. The trick is to think of tricks. Just imagine them. You know my buddy runs the fish fry next door, and I was over there one day, and he says to me, 'How can I make more money doing this?' I told him I'd show him the next day. So, I took a piece of wood he uses for the fire, went home and cut out small fishes, painted them green and toasted them. Then I just nailed them to a long board, brought it back to him the next day, told him to sell it for fifty-four dollars. I was like, 'How much do you think this wood cost you?' He thought maybe thirty cents." Fred's eyes widened at his own disbelief.

"That's a huge profit margin! My buddy put it on the wall, and some retired woman took it home the next day! See, you've just got to be creative. That's why I don't need to work for anyone. All that these corporations do is hold you down, limit your finances..." He continued to ramble nonsensically about things I can't recall. Somehow, he got to mentioning his "smoking hot wife," providing me reassurance that he wasn't hitting on me in front of my mom.

"You just have to go after what you want. I'll tell you I was quite the ladies' man when I was young. I play almost every instrument you can think of, and I am quite a good singer as well."

"Really? I sing too," I added hoping to twist his ranting into a conversation.

"Yeah, I bet I could clear a room faster than you," he said coyly, leaning into my bubble.

"What, are you trying to make me go neek at the wees?" I turned to my mom to share in my tongue-tied embarrassment, "Wow, you're really doing a great job!" I added, attempting a graceful recovery. He carried on unfazed by my interjection.

"Oh, I was a stud. But, then I got into a bad accident that sliced my cerebral cortex, lost a lot of hair, and was told I couldn't walk again." My mom's jaw drop; my eyes widened.

"And I just thought, 'How dare you judge me by your limitations,' I was determined to walk again. And they said, 'No, no you can't.' They measured every biometric they could and told me it wasn't possible. But you know what? They couldn't measure my desire." Shaking his head with a mischievous look, he repeated with greater gumption,

"They can measure every system, every metric, but they can't measure my desire. See? That's what life's about: desire. So, I met this banging girl and asked her to dinner. She already had a date that night, but I said, 'No. This is really important. Come to dinner with me.' Of course, she eventually said yes, canceled her date, and we went to dinner. The whole time we kept bouncing questions back and forth like: Do you like honey-mustard? Where did you grow up? What's your favorite movie? We laughed until we cried! The whole time. And at the end, I was like, 'So do you want to marry me or what?' She said yes, we were married nine days later and have been married for twenty-eight years. I am more in love with her today than the day we met!"

"It's funny, on our first date, I surprised her—took her to the beach for a picnic. But that wasn't the best part. She loved it so much I bought the land for her! And on our tenth anniversary, I had gone to that beach and spent ten minutes on each side sketching a lighthouse. I built it for her; a three-hundred-thousand-dollar lighthouse! And you know what? The crystal is the same crystal from a St. Petersburg Lighthouse in Russia."

I had to interrupt. "Wait, what? Now, how do you do something like that?"

"You just take it. I rented a truck, drove over the border at night, and prayed no one caught me!"

"Wow, unbelievable," I shook my head in amazement or perhaps disbelief. I hadn't decided yet.

Chuckling to himself, "Yeah, I have lived a good life."

"So what's the secret?" Heading towards some great crossroads in my life, I had to know how he arrived at fifty-four-years-old with such rare admiration and enthusiasm for life.

"It's easy. Here it is: you're going to come to forks in the road many times in your life." He slammed his wrists together and opened his hands, emphasizing the two different directions we often need to decide between.

"It doesn't matter which way you go. It really doesn't, you just have to go! Don't wait; pick one right now and go! Run down that path because if you don't, someone else will and will beat you to it. The first personal growth book that was ever written changed my life and is the reason I am where I am today. Have you heard of the book 'Think and Grow Rich?'"

"By Nap—"

"Napoleon Hill."

"Yes."

"Have you read it?"

"No."

"Read it. And understand it. Do it."

"Okay."

"It has the secret to everything you need to know. If you understand it, you will be successful. I can tell you'll be very successful. You have what it takes, but get rid of that nose ring—now."

I nodded my head slowly as if I was considering this old-man's advice.

"Seriously, get rid of it. You will be very successful but not if you don't take out that ring. It is losing you more opportunities than you know."

"I'll think about it," I said, trying to avoid getting defensive. What did he know about my life?

"Anyway, you've got to create opportunities too. There was this one time I went down to Florida with some buddies. We had no money, no jobs. We rented an empty bus station to stay in and right across the street there was this filling station with a 'help wanted' sign. So, I went over and said, 'Hey, you're looking for help. What do you do here?' They were a full-service filling station, so I said, 'I'm your man. I can pump gas, wash cars, whatever else you need I'll pick it up, just show me once!' So, I got the job, made some business cards, and handed them out to people who drove in with nice cars. I told them I'd detail their car on the weekend, and eventually, they set me up with business connections."

Time passed, and I could no longer tell if we had been standing there for five minutes or thirty minutes. The sun, without fail, continued to move towards the western horizon. Eager to experience our last sunset in Fish Creek, my mom, who once was emotionally invested in the conversation, tired and drew away in an attempt to drag us along towards the checkout counter. We slowly followed suit.

"You know, no one taught me this stuff I discovered it on my own. If you mix navy and white together, you get this beautiful gray! I was so excited that I created the color, I told my buddy, and he was like, 'Well, yeah. I learned that in second grade.' But I discovered it." The rims of his lips rose with great pride.

"Here. This is it!" He stopped and grabbed a horizontal beach painting that was displayed in the canoe set in the center of the room for efficient decor.

"Isn't that beautiful?" Fred's astonishment at his own creation gave me a new perspective—he discovered these colors in nature and brought them to life. Flipping the painting over, he said,

"Look. See it's me before my accident. Wasn't I a handsome man?" Next to the picture, he included a small biography with his signature. The same signature hangs in our living room, but now with more significance. We finally returned to the counter to purchase the notecards and hurry out.

"Yeah, so I have really lived a good life. How old are you?" He asked with great excitement.

"Twenty-one."

He stopped. "Oh, you do not know how good it gets!" The conviction in his body language and tone soaked into the depressions of my hopes and dreams reinforcing that they are not foolish but still so possible.

"Are you married?"

"No."

"Do you have a boyfriend?"

"No."

"What?! Why not?" He asked in that tone no single person appreciates.

"I don't know. I just don't. There's not really anyone I want to date," I stated, not even convincing myself.

"Oh, you've got to get one. Do you go to the gym?"

"Haha, no," I admitted with no shame.

"Do it. I'll tell you why. You'll meet motivated people there. Anyway, get a boyfriend. And you want to know the secret to keeping one? Be a phenomenal kisser; learn how to kiss." Honest advice from a fifty-four-year-old ladies' man.

"You have no idea what's yet to come!"

"Thanks, Fred." I leaned over the counter with my hand stretched out. He grabbed my hand with that same fervor for life,

"Good luck. Take out that nose ring."

I smiled in acknowledgment and turned towards the door.

"That's a great handshake you have!"

I looked over my right shoulder playfully, "I know."

I walked out those doors as if it was any other store. But Fred's stories and insights, although possibly a figment of his own imagination, inspired me more than any job, person, or event that whole year. His passion for life, simple perspective, and belief in me stirred my visions, heightening their possibility, and feeding my hunger for a purpose and a plan.

When I came home to St. Paul the next day, I set my luggage in my room and stood in front of my dresser mirror that had reflected every change in me since I was two-years-old. The possibility of everything I could be and do overwhelmed me. As Fred's words continued to filter through everything I once thought I knew, I looked at my nose ring for the first time with disdain. I questioned the authority and grounds for his belief but more strongly questioned the reality of mine. If he was right, that my nose ring was stopping me from opportunities I didn't even know about, regardless of whether that was fair or not, then I was the fool. I took it out slowly, then all at once. As I did, I took another step closer to realizing my full potential and took a deep breath to officiate a new chapter.

———

I'll let heaven rule my thoughts and choose my dreams for I am incapable of such wonders.

Ramblings

We overcomplicate life, we under examine ourselves, we leave things broken, we enter things that haven't started. We beat on questioning our questions. We see things the way we want to see them. We carry everyone's weight; we don't let go of our own. And in time we realize we know not what we're doing.

But we must know that we are blessed. Let us be bold in our dreams, weak in our assumptions, wise in our undertakings. May our hearts rejoice with others and weep with their sorrows. Let us give until we break, love until it hurts, and pray until our knees give out, then pray some more—for that is the only way to participate in the fullness of life.

Dad

"I wanted to be a railroad engineer..." he said as he leaned back against the grill of the conversion van that had carried us over mountains and bridges and stretches of desert and forest. My father is a man molded by the logistics of life, sporting worn housework jeans through it all. As a child, his father was active in personal pursuits—bowling leagues, church choir, and social groups. Clarence was a popular man for these things, though arguably we all can be if we devote our lives to social endeavors. Regardless, with his wife, Ione, and their children Cheryl, John, and my dad, Craig, they lived a simple life. Ione worked primarily in the kitchen cooking meals she'd rather not eat and spent her down time cleaning the three-bedroom, split-level home they owned just blocks away from the local high school. These were the sixties and seventies when kids still walked to school and played outside late into the evening without parental concern. Though parents did worry about other things—Ione found a bag of weed in John's room and asked my dad if John was gay. He wasn't, and my grandma's concern was alleviated and they continued on with their semi-normal lives in shades of yellow, green, and jean until Clarence was diagnosed with Leukemia. Unfortunately, the disease plagued his system faster than medical advancements leaving Clarence with only a hope of survival. After blood transfusions and a weakened immune system, pneumonia won. My dad faced high school without the strength of his father, and fatherhood without Clarence's example. And so, the decisions of my own dad were resolved with the fear of going on without his.

My dad turned against his ambitions to support a greater one—fatherhood. Although his summers at Grandma's farmhouse in Staples taught him the alluring life of railroad men as they called to him in passing or when they sought food from the house, the dreamer realized his financial and personal obligations to his future family could not be met by this captivating career. And so, Craig followed in his father's ways and pursued electrical engineering. Technical school proved to be enough to work for Honeywell designing aircraft and spacecraft technology. Yet, the industry itself couldn't support his position for any longer than it took to receive his degree. From job to job, Craig moved about maximizing his potential only to be laid off as an unaffordable expense for companies. He was relentless in his commitment to support his greatest goal.

Staring into the driveway he had personally stripped and repaved, he continued,

"...But I needed to choose something more suitable to have a family. It's definitely been hard on your mom and me to pull everything off, but, it's okay," he shrugged, "our goal is to give you kids everything you want and need." I could tell when my dad was suppressing tears, but I couldn't tell if this time it was because of the suffering he had packed away for decades or because of the fruits of those very sufferings.

"This life is hard. Some would say it is hell on earth and I believe it. This place sucks. There's a far better place for us, but I think we're here for a reason. My goal is to make it to heaven, and everything else means nothing. I'm okay with the thought of dying, but I don't think I will anytime soon. Honestly, I think my purpose is to be here for Philip." I nodded slowly in agreement with my father, whom up to this point, I took for a man without the contemplation of purpose or death, but rather a man who studied lawn care methods and physics principles for their practical applications around the house. His insight and honesty overwhelmed me. I was his little princess, but I was not his reason for being. He stood in a new light. This light illuminated his figure as I bathed in this beautiful reality that we both clearly recognized and accepted, and admired the faithful angel that my dad became for his suffering son.

Philip bore great burdens when I was too young to conceive of their weight, and the few brushes I had against his yoke are too raw to relive through words. But that time was only a season of Philip's life. And as seasons come and go, closing one period of time, and leading to the next, so do the seasons of our lives. Philip eventually, slowly and then somehow all of a sudden, stretched out and breathed again into another sphere of living. So, while my dad's purpose may have been to help Philip in his season of suffering—a theory I find overwhelmingly convincing—I cannot help but think his purpose is not fully lived out. For we all serve a grand purpose: to love and know God as he is in heaven and to obey that which he commands for the sake of our holiness. But when that grand purpose is broken down into years within a lifetime, weeks within a year, days within a week, we begin to see the small callings to sainthood more clearly and how they compound for the fulfillment of our greater purpose. And so, my dad was the hero through Philip's trials, and I am confident he will continue to be used by God for years to come.

To Rest in Your Spirit

Dear Jesus: I want to rest in your most Holy Spirit and dream of your love with the taste of Heaven on my lips and a song of praise in my heart. For if tonight I return home to you, I will count myself blessed, but if you choose to keep me here another day, I will strive so eagerly to attain your perfect love in my thoughts and in every word and deed, bringing Heaven closer to Earth all for your greater glory.

I praise you in the quiet depths of my heart and long for you to be present like oxygen. For it is you that sustains my very being. All I long for is to come to know you more, and by knowing you, love you, and by loving you, draw closer to our perfect union.

Alex

Alex is my brother, and I love him, and it is hard to love him. Our early relationship was a mix of sentiments.

I remember being his alarm clock in high school. I'd cross the hall four different times trying to wake him up. He would roll over in bed, unconcerned about time or my morning schedule. Frustrated, I would flip on his ceiling light switch, flooding his square bedroom with unnerving yellow light. Behind me, I would slam the hollow wooden door—not exactly earth shattering but loud enough to get the point across.

I remember talking with him about girls while tearing the weeds out of our lawn. As dirt clotted beneath our fingernails, we would share complaints about the summer heat and our tedious chores, and he would offer details about his life and the type of girls he liked—the real ones, not the annoying, shallow, ditzy type.

I remember being blatantly ignored by him in the hallway at school. He'd acknowledge a wall over me. It was annoying, but he often had more important objects of his attention—like the two girls whose hands were interwoven with his as they strutted to class.

I remember the times we hung out with no distracting computers or phones or video games. He would excitedly participate in my amusements, like my offer to give him five dollars if he let me adorn him in my new, flowery Easter dress, matching hat, and heels. The hallway became his runway and I gave him a matching purse.

In college, I evidently felt the shift in sibling relationship dynamics. No longer could I walk across the hall to yell at him to turn down the music or make light conversation in the car on the way to school. We didn't eat at the same dinner table or cross paths in the same living room. At that point, our relationship had to become intentional if we were to remain in contact with one another. So, I made it a point to visit him in his dorm room or have lunch together when we shared the same college campus. We became friends in a way I had never expected. I actually wanted to check in on him and care for him. At the same time, Alex was transitioning too. He was adjusting to a new academic world and a new lifestyle with greater responsibilities. He wasn't adjusting well, and it began to take a toll.

Crossroads

We come to a crossroads clouded in darkness through to its end. We know not what lies on one road or the other that diverges away, only that both are a loss of something and a gain of another. The dark may fade on the road we neglected—we peer through the trees to see what we missed, only still to be in darkness on the path we've already chosen.

As Fred once told me, none of that matters. It doesn't matter how many directions there are before you, for you still must choose one. We must move in either direction; it doesn't matter which. Just choose one and move assuredly, trusting that you only knew what you knew when you knew it and made the most prudent decision you could afford. I don't know if this sound advice.

I don't know a lot of things lately, and it showers doubt over me. Doubt seeps into my clothes with heavy self-consciousness. We have one life with multiple chances to get this life right. But with time as a construct, multiple chances—although a good teacher they are—steal effort away from happiness. I feel I need to get it right. I have one life to become a saint, and I want to do something meaningful, joyful, and specific to my talents and abilities. The clock ticks mockingly, and I wonder what I'm not doing.

Lord, I must trust you. I have no idea what I am doing. I don't know where you want me to go.

———

These moments of doubt and unrest are the bait for truth. For the more I think I know, the more I fail to know.

Risks and Rewards

They say with great risks come great rewards. I believe it. I stocked shelves and had pseudo-authority to override check-out lane operations and sit-in on leadership meetings at Target. I enjoyed these duties of customer—or in the eyes of Target, guest—service. Those nine months had added a wealth of experience and knowledge to an already heavy sales background. Yet, my foresight could never reconcile the path of a Store Executive. The picture that I painted was uninspiring and dull. It certainly wouldn't have been the worst path—it's a great career for many who are energized by the work, but that didn't include me. And so, I sought an escape.

Around the same time, I curiously attended a College Republicans meeting—though primarily I was in search of free pizza and secondarily there to appease my friend Kathleen who was a board member of the campus group. I assumed a Republican title due to my religious leanings and conservative understanding of our government's origins, purpose, and role. So, I sat in a University of St. Thomas classroom among activists, my-parents-are-Republicans, the well-connected, and the disengaged (like myself). Representative Tara Mack—a young, petite, blonde with a superb fashion sense—walked through the door with the Chair of the group, Andrew. He proceeded to introduce her at the front of the room. She stood firmly as if on the floor of the House Chamber and spoke about recent happenings within the Legislature, political strategy, and the misguided principles of "the other side of the aisle." She highlighted her fellow Republicans' priorities and how they were working to see them through. She pronounced the importance of young perspectives in government. She opened up the sky, and I saw its capacity, its limitlessness.

Its limitlessness stayed with me and drew me to my computer that evening. In my career confusion, with six months before college graduation, I sat on my bed within the four colorful bedroom walls in my college house, searching the internet for internship opportunities at the Minnesota House of Representatives. By the Lord's great will, I found a program. I emailed Representative Mack asking if I could be her intern, and a few months later, I stepped out onto that icy Capitol pavement to navigate my way through the State Office Building to Tara Mack's office on the third floor. I had no idea what I was in for, what my role would be, what I would need to know, or how I would be able to do this. I had no expectations, except that I was capable of accepting whatever would come my way because the Lord had guided me to that intern desk.

Compass

Put down the compass, fold up the map, and walk forward with a quiet heart, open eyes, and be attentive to the forces that beckon you onward. Do not direct yourself, only follow the faith you employed with your first step. Have faith that you are where you are meant to be, you are where God wants to love you best, you are in a place of God's intention. Keep walking. Trust in him, and he will do the rest.

That Which Fires the Soul

I have yet to figure out what will make me most happy and fulfilled. But on the days I do fool myself into thinking I have finally gotten it, I am essentially most happy. To idealize a profession wherein our greatest desires and dreams unfold within our imagination is to awaken the heart to its potential.

Such potential has been realized to be frightening. I was considering a role in politics: a career that could be long or short-lived, I could walk away humiliated and degraded or uplifted and accomplished, my time could be wasted on petty politics or game-changing policy. These considerations scared me. Even so, that wasn't my greatest fear. It wasn't that I might not be up for the fight, inadequate, or unknowledgeable. My greatest fear was that I could be wonderfully brilliant. It is truly possible that my (or anyone's) career could be fundamentally corrective for the nation. People could vote for me for national office and experience my decision-making ability. World leaders could know me and love me and trust me and respect me. My greatest fear is that it is all possible.

For those of us who believe in Christ, it truly is all possible (Mark 9:23). And when what is possible for us is frightening, we must run towards it. For that is when we have discovered a passion and interest that can awaken us to our great potential, a potential worth discovering.

Differences

Despite my new opportunity, I decided to continue working in retail through the end of the school year in case my political endeavor was only a phase.

One evening that winter, I closed the store with an intriguingly charming guy named Paul. Paul was no exceptional looker or leader at first introduction, but he had a quiet sincerity and genuine smile that embraced everyone. I was curious about the boy and grateful to have the opportunity to work more closely with him. While we worked the aisles, straightening and organizing their contents, school and work cluttered our conversation. I mentioned my excitement to be partaking in the legislative session next spring, and his enthusiasm grew as he commented on his experience working for Obama's 2012 presidential campaign on his campus in Wisconsin.

We began discussing issues that rested at the top of our consciousness, and he dared to venture into specifics.

"So," he said still processing his succeeding word choice, his hands purposefully arranging picture frames in their precise locations, "you—we—must be one the same side then." His hesitation grew as I tried to digest his political ideology within seconds, a path I cautioned at work.

"Well, are you an elephant or a donkey? I'm an elephant," I said, avoiding the plain terms. His eyes rolled upward as he searched for understanding,

"Really?" He responded, "Huh—I mean, I'm a donkey. I guess I'm surprised." So was I. Sure I hadn't previously judged his political preference, but I didn't see how he could've judged mine given the shallowness of any previous conversation. But somehow he did, and I was completely offended. Just kidding, I was rather satisfied by the political ambiguity wherein our discussion of the issues didn't resort to typical talking points of either side.

The conversation ensued. The first few steps were over eggshells as we tried to measure the political intensity of the other which we both found to be sincere and informed. But the maturity in which we presented our ideas, philosophies, and questions impressed my own expectations. Throughout the next hour, as we worked into the bedding and storage aisles, we challenged one another and found ourselves in agreement with the principle and importance of social welfare—if managed well and appropriately, which we both agreed had not yet been done, and I argued further will likely never be done at a federal level considering the size of the United States. I like to think he was surprised, too, by the caliber of the discussion and the depth of humanity explored in his conversation with a Republican, discussion the media has tried to hide from the public.

It is moments like those—dialogue between two of the more earnest of the parties—that remind me that we're not that different.

Much of our desires are the same. And my hope is renewed in the potential for civilization to rightly orient politics.

ROMANCE

I want passionate, blazing romance. The kind that never dies. Flirt with me until you take your final rest. Love me until you take your last breath. Sometimes I fear it is only actors and actresses who know of these things I long for. Yet I know love is created by God; God is love. Furthermore, I trust the Lord's love for me grows each day as I live rightly or not, humbly or not, generously or not. I believe he longs for me in blank spaces of time. And although God's love cannot compare to man, such love does exist. Therefore, I can hope for it. And I will work for it all the days of my life. To grow with you, to grow into you, to be one with you. Fight with me but do not forget to fight for me. May we argue about china patterns and bills but never about the existence of love and compassion, for my heart is too fragile and your pride too deep. Together we will show the world the love Christ has for us, the care he pours into our souls. May we be examples for our children of how to love. Please take the burden of this goal and pray for us, oh Love, whom I know not.

The Twenty-Four Hour Rule

Emotions can be beautiful and ugly. We can easily get caught up in their pleasures that both destroy and create, and our minds blindly lose track of the truth of the matter. We act rashly.

One night, after an hour decompression conversation about our futures, I admitted to Courtney, while we sat in my room—I sulking on my ironically so-called loveseat—that I wanted to call Cole. As an old friend who manipulatively knew me inside and out, I believed he'd offer comforting words—and perhaps other complimentary tones my heart longed to hear again, including his voice. She advised me to sleep on it and wait twenty-four hours before calling him.

"This will give you time to think it through and if you still feel it's important tomorrow, go ahead and call him," she said as I instinctively disagreed. *I am going to feel the same way tomorrow, I* insisted.

Not even twenty-four hours later, when I awoke the next day, I found to my dismay my emotions had been soothed by sleep's potion. I was no longer insistent on my dependence on him, though I wish I still had a reason to call him; my vision cleared and I could anticipate reality—the probability of disappointment, regret, and embarrassment of an inappropriate phone call.

Though twenty-four hours would save my heart from trouble many times, Cole's power still lorded over me.

Thief

It's amazing where love can lead you then leave you. I told him I'd always love him. Maybe it truly will last, but maybe it won't. Waking to a text from a friend asking which professor I had for Business Ethics began a true awakening of the reality of Cole.

"I, maybe, kinda, am not using your paper you wrote on Cole for my class," Jack texted back after learning we didn't have the same professors. Cole had given Jack the paper I wrote earlier that year—the one I wrote after meeting him for a drink at Wild Bill's—to use for the same project. The more I thought about it, the madder I got. I am not a cheater. I don't condone it. And worse, that term paper was freely handed out by another person—the very person I interviewed on business ethics. By no means did Cole have the right to give away my work for someone else's use.

Not wanting to make a big deal out of something that most people don't think twice about, I simply texted Cole:

"I'm disappointed you'd encourage someone to rip off my work, especially without asking me." I received no response for twelve hours. I wasn't surprised by his lack of confrontation or apology. He never had a gentleman's way and didn't work to secure one. I had to breathe deeply to prevent myself from being passive aggressive or blowing my emotions out of proportion. After rationalizing the situation, I texted him again:

"...and that you couldn't even muster a sincere apology." I was biting my tongue to restrain the things I couldn't take back, though I did add the clapping hands emoji. I couldn't help myself. Within minutes he texted back:

"I didn't want to text you an apology and forgot to call you this afternoon. But I am very sorry. I never meant to disappoint you. I was just trying to help Jack, and I did ask him to talk to you. It never even crossed my mind that you wouldn't want me to send it to him. Again, I am truly sorry."

He offered a seemingly sincere apology, and I accepted it with an honest, "Thank you," but I wouldn't accept any of the excuses with which he ladened the text. I have always known that time is love—if one doesn't make time for you, one doesn't care to make the time. It's simple. His excuses were unmoving, and my distaste for him grew. This time, I saw Chris clearly. I had finally accepted him for who he was or at least, who he was in relation to me.

Cole couldn't ever give me what I needed. His belated and coerced text apology was all time and care he could muster. At one point, I meant more to him than that. At one point, I was the twinkle and apple of his eye, the jump in his step. And he, he was the clock that woke me up, the poetry that ran through my head without welcome or plea. He was the hope and the nurturer of butterflies. He was the one that knew me before I knew myself.

I had never known love like that before—if I can even call it that, and it tortured me ruthlessly. I told him I'd love him forever and I truly believed that. But I was perpetually waiting for his; I was waiting for something that I could never have.

It was then I recognized loss and the way memories creep joyfully into sight while their unwelcome arrival wets the watercolor masterpiece into a gray cloud of confusion and disillusion which left me wondering if I ever truly had his heart, and if not, how I could lose something I never had.

The Walk Home

He approached me confidently with his arm read
and his intentions set on dancing.

"I want to dance with you," he said as he pu
the pillar I was leaning against. Appreciative of hi
joined him on the dance floor. He took my hand in hi
other around the small of my back as we drew closer to ᵤnother. He
danced well, with the kind of affection seldom received at a bar, twirling
me out and drawing me back in.

After a few dances, he asked if I wanted to "get out of here," but
I wouldn't leave without Elizabeth who was strapped to our friend Tony.
The four of us left Plums, the neighborhood Thursday-night-bar, in
search for a cab on a bitter winter night. For reasons I can't recall, the
boys decided to come home with Elizabeth and me. So, the cab pulled
up to our front door, and a curious night ensued.

Matt followed me up to my room. I folded clothes that had been
strewn on my bed in an attempt to find the perfect outfit that night and
hung them within the overcrowded hole in the wall I called my closet.
He sat on my couch, arms and legs stretched out casually, asking me
questions and surveying the pictures on my wall. As 3:00 a.m. rolled
around, my patience grew thin, and I mustered the courage to suggest
we sleep in separate beds. I brought him into my absent roommate's
room and began to prepare the bed for him.

"I just think it's a good idea if you sleep in here," I mentioned.
He clearly wasn't having it. Groaning and noticeably battling conflicting
thoughts he said, more to himself than me,

"I am not sleeping in this crappy room." He paced the path from
the bed to the door as I watched him stitch together the feelings of
disappointment and rage into words.

"What's the problem?" I begged, seeking his genuine emotions.

"I just—I don't want to."

"Fine."

He sat on the edge of the bed next to me and laid back with his
hands on his face as if he could disappear from this place. I could feel
his inaudible humility, and I filled in the blanks of his silence.

d you think you were going to get laid tonight?" I asked, ed by my own inexperienced instinct and courageously blunt estion.

"Kinda," he responded with his hands still covering his face.

"Did I give you that impression?" I asked impatiently, but also earnestly, sincerely hoping I hadn't.

"No."

"Okay, well, you can either crash in here, or you can go home if you'd like," I suggested, thinking the latter might be the easiest and less traumatic option for the both of us.

He sat up.

"I think I am going to go home."

I paused, waiting to see if he'd at least ask for my number. He didn't. "Okay, I think that's a good idea."

Elizabeth entered as if on cue.

"Yeah, I'm in my pajama set," she pointed out, breaking down in dance in the doorway.

"And I have got some sweet sweats," Tony chimed in from the other end of the hallway, showing off Elizabeth's sweatpants that missed the floor by six inches.

"Great look," I sarcastically admitted as I went into my room next-door to grab Matt's coat.

I walked him downstairs to show him the door. As he put on his boots, I watched him, curious of what to say or if he'd ever ask for my number. He tied his shoelaces as if trying to stall time, and the awkward silence slowly escalated. My stomach churned with discomfort knowing this boy was presuming a night from me that he never deserved.

"Perhaps we'll see each other again," Matt said, tying the laces of the boots that would carry him to his own bed that night.

"If fate allows," I added, knowing it could be due to nothing else without my number or even last name to find me on Facebook (a tool I frequently took advantage of).

"Fate's a dangerous thing."

"Fate's a good thing."

He stood up and looked in my eyes as if trying to find his next move buried inside them.

"Well, goodnight," I said.

"Yeah, goodnight."

I locked the door behind him and shook the disgust from my backbone that had moments earlier come in handy. As I walked the steep staircase back upstairs, I recounted the various steps of the night that led Matt back to his house. I was stunned by my strength and determination to protect our hearts. Lacking experience in such presumptuous circumstances, I knew the Holy Spirit poured great wisdom into my heart as I pursued holiness. And as I laid in bed alone that night, I realized moments like those are the ones that define us, making us weaker or stronger, more restless or whole. With every decision, we mark our journey towards or away from love. I will always choose to move towards love. And because of it, I can hope in its fullness in me and I in it.

I will find great love one day with someone who knows my worth and honors me with the highest regard. I will find great love one day.

The following day, I may not have found love, but a letter that had been wedged in the handle of our outdoor screen door addressed to me. Recognizing the misspelling of my name, I both hoped and feared it was from the guy from last night. I was anxious to open the letter for I didn't know what to expect or what I wanted to find within that white envelope.

> "Hey Clare,
> I am sorry if I was rude or presumptuous last night.
> Let me know if you ever want to play guitar,
> Matt Sweeney
> 651-555-6758"

As much as the memory of the night made me uncomfortable and consequently indifferent to seeing him again, I believed Matt deserved to be recognized for his humility and maturity. For I respect a handwritten note above any text message, even if it was indeed his only option at that point to speak to me again. So, I texted him with my gratitude and avoided ever seeing him again.

Sick

After arriving at our family's house we so rarely visited, I hopped out of the front seat of the mighty conversion van and headed towards the back of the truck to grab the load of food my mom had picked up for my sick aunt and her family. I grabbed a veggie platter, pizza, and bag full of other goodies and challenged myself to enter their home without fear. I hadn't seen Aunt Kim in over a year; more importantly, I hadn't seen her since she was diagnosed with Leukemia. Really, I had never visited a sick family member in my memorable years. Because of such inexperience, interacting with Kim seemed daunting as I navigated the selection of words to express what is expected or appreciated or necessary.

My cousin Andrea answered the door with food in her mouth as her car warmed up in the driveway. She greeted me warmly but casually as I slipped one boot off after the other and walked up the split staircase to the war zone. Uncle Eric, Aunt Kim, and Cousin Mathias stood awkwardly in opposing places around the island in their kitchen. They barely made eye contact as I began to take off my coat, slowly regretting my assumption that we would visit long enough to make that sensible. Kim feebly picked up her small dog and held him lightly in her arms. Eric moved about the kitchen with unassured intention. Seeming like a safer option, I turned to greet him first while my mom made a distraction entering their home. The hug was awkward and forced; I began to sense something wasn't quite right, as if my mom and I had walked into a secret.

Yet, for them, Eric said, that's how things had been for their grieving family as they watched the life being doped out of their lives. Aunt Kim was unemotional, withdrawn, and unrecognizable. He was lost in her too; hopelessly.

We left only a few minutes later, surely having had little effect in lifting their burden. I gained another human experience that so frequently presents itself to the loved ones of sufferers, eternally profiting us who suffer with another, care for another, and make sacrifices for another. That suffering might be meaningful is a rather beautiful, and rather old idea. Jesus himself demonstrates this through a death he did not ask for; he suffered, and we gained life. Though Aunt

Kim's suffering was undeniably painful for her and her loved ones, Kim's suffering was a blessed opportunity for us to care for another. She provided us an opportunity to give of ourselves, though I can hardly count myself in that group of caretakers.

India

I was dreaming of adventurous things to do, and India struck my heart. My memory fails to remind me how India first crossed the endless scope of my imagination, but however it got there, the idea stirred it with questions and wonderment of a new world wherein the only reason I could think not to go was "Why not?" I knew nothing of the land or its people—that's what made it so inviting. As I explored the potentiality of visiting and serving this eastern country, my desire for the experience grew deeper.

I shared this aspiration with my roommate, Elizabeth, who mentioned that at our school a service organization called VISION was taking a trip there in three months. The timing was providential, and the Lord sent me to India.

I had never milked a cow, and for some reason decided it was an important life experience. To my surprise, across from the two-story colorful house that I would call my home for three weeks was an open shelter for Ramesh's cows. Cows are sacred to Indians, so although they are essential for obtaining milk, Indians don't eat the cows. Since the bulls, or, male cows, cannot provide meat or milk, owning one is a sign of prestige and honor. If the running water in the house wasn't a giveaway, the bull in Ramesh's pen told of the gentleman's education and trade. Fittingly, Ramesh named his bull Prince Charles, and his female counterpart, Queen Elizabeth. To this follower of the collusion of world powers, the name for their offspring was appropriate—Barak Obama, the forty-fourth President of the United States of America. Seeing an opportunity to not only milk a cow but Queen Elizabeth, I asked our new friends at iSpiice (Integrated Social Programs in Indian Child Education) who were the tenants of Ramesh's first floor, if I could.

Ask and you shall receive, or, in this case, keep asking and eventually they'll say, "Yes, you can milk the cow."

After a few days of pressuring the guys, Ravi led me outside over the flowers planted ornately along the driveway and down into the shelter in which Ramesh housed his farming equipment and his fire pit. The pit was a deep rectangular cement hole in which he laid stray branches vertically, resting them against the walls of the pit. Ramesh sat looking out towards his growing crop with the fire burning fervently at his feet. Ravi said something unintelligible to Ramesh and turned to me in broken English,

"OK, now ask." Although Ravi hadn't prepped me for this impromptu meeting, I warily attempted to greet Ramesh in their native tongue.

"मेरा नाम Claire है." No, I don't know how to read that either. I meant to say, "Meraa naam Claire hai." Although it probably sounded to them like "adlcs amff Claire adf." Besides, it was pointless; Ramesh spoke fluent English. He said,

"Hello," with the quick head-tilt that implied both "yes" and "no" and apparently, anything else they wanted. Ravi prompted me to ask, motioning his hand toward Ramesh.

"Can I milk your cow?" I asked with enthusiasm and a bit of fear not knowing how enthused he would be about the idea.

"Yes. Yes," he replied emphatically, then rose slowly from his seat. "Come. Come."

Ravi and I followed him up to the driveway where he led me to his livestock. He motioned towards the cow.

"Go on, try it," he pushed. I grabbed those utters and pulled.

"Yes, like that," he acknowledged. The cows had already been milked that morning so he said I could come back the next morning at 7:00 a.m. to do the job.

That following morning, Shane came into the women's quarters and loudly whispered my name through the dark.

"It's time to milk the cows," he eagerly pronounced. I rose from my new down-sleeping bag I picked up the week earlier in anticipation of sleeping in the mountains and zipped up the purple sweatshirt from the thrift store I later regretted buying. We went out and greeted Ramesh.

"Good morning Ramesh. How are you?"

"Good," he said in his thick accent, still buried in his newspaper.

"We're ready to milk Queen Elizabeth."

"Good," he again responded.

"What's happening in the world?"

"News, always news," he said folding the newspaper to go let the cows out of their stables. Ramesh's wife tossed feed into the permanent basin and out came Prince Charles. Then came Barak Obama and Queen Elizabeth. His wife spent time prepping Queen Elizabeth's utter—wiping off the dung and applying a fatty lubricant.

"Go!" Ramesh said, motioning to the cow. I followed orders and bent down next to his wife to help. Without using words, she first drew her hands down the utter, demonstrating the motion. I nodded my head enthusiastically and took over. I pulled and pulled and pulled and pulled and stopped. I don't know if I was nervous about the professional squatting right next to me or the audience I had behind me, but I decided it was enough to check it off my bucket list. In retrospect, I should have milked the whole thing and given his wife a day off from her duties that I found so exciting, but I didn't and joined Ramesh by his fire.

We talked about life—his was simple. He woke, showered, ate, and cared for his animals, and sat by his fire. I suggested it must be a peaceful life and he agreed. He has a daughter and son and one wife. He began learning English in the sixth grade. He studied geography in school so he knew where Minnesota could be found on a map. We talked about the weather, and he was interested in the weather at home. He was also interested in my family. I asked him if he had been to the US and he said he hadn't and never wanted to. I told him I didn't blame him. He went on to say that the US shouldn't be involved in so many global affairs, that it is too powerful. I agreed. He said the US, like Delhi, is too "hustle-bustle" and too interested in money. I agreed, remarking that those things only make them unhappier. He laughed, nodding his head as he got up to add another log to the fire. He told me about his farming and that he enjoyed it and that he would be dying soon. He seemed to have accepted it and was planning on finishing his life in peace. Ramesh had built his dwelling and rented the lower half to Varun and his organization, iSpiice. He only bought his calf's grandmother, and the rest have grown with him and supported him and his crop. He seemed happy. He offered me a cigarette, and I declined, recalling the rules of the group, though I would normally have thrown caution to the wind and done what the Romans do—or Indians do. Still, he insisted; I resisted. He gave up and sat back again. We continued the dialogue of strangers as the fire warmed the cool air around us and the mountains became alive with the sunrise before us.

Every evening, our group would form a circle in the girls' room as best as possible—three on each bed, a few on the floor—and we would talk about our days and experiences and lives. During one reflection on spirituality, Shane mentioned he wanted to be the person these people—the Indians we were serving—could count on instead of looking to a higher power for consolation. He believed that the only thing one can count on in life is the physical, human person. I recognized this philosophy in contrast to a Christian's who believes we suffer because we depend on worldly consolations—such as people and things or our health and environment, and that suffering is meant to reaffirm our covenant with the Lord—that he is our sole protector and comforter, the one whom we can always trust. So, I sat in the small bedroom in a circle with my companions and friends hearing Shane's words and grimaced as I thought Jesus might have at the sound of this illusion. My heart breaks for those who feel they have nothing more to lean on than a human shoulder, nothing more to offer than their human limitations. And still, I wondered how those children felt, the children who live barefoot in dirty rainwater. From whom would they seek consolation?

Regardless, we offered what consolations we could, whether one sees that as mere human work or the grace of God. We taught computer and English classes, painted daycares, and tutored students.

Varun would take a small group of us every afternoon to a daycare that was a short walk into a village. One of those days, he remained with us, standing there in the center of the daycare cluttered with paint buckets and old classroom furniture watching us stroke the walls—some of us doing it more delicately than others. Varun was quiet and contemplative. I decided to ask him about the caste system which had been explained to me in various religion classes, but not yet from "the devil's mouth," and he explained sufficiently. I then asked which caste he was a part of, and he only responded that he didn't believe in the system, only to later admit that his parents were the Kshatriyas, the warriors. I asked if he believed in God or gods and he said he didn't. Satisfied with the information he offered, I continued painting the alphabet on the daycare wall as he stood behind and watched us. A few minutes later he broke the silence.

"What faith are you?" he asked casually. I told him Catholic/Christian.

"Are you familiar with Christianity?"

"Yeah," he said with indifferent composition. The goats in the surrounding village fields groaned nonchalantly as I dipped my paint brush into a bowl of green paint.

"Do you know the parents of Jesus?" he asked without inflection, furthering the ambiguity of the elementary question.

"Yeah, Mary and Joseph?"

"Yeah," with a challenging rise in his tone he prodded, "Virgin Mary?"

"Yeah...?"

He broke the obscurity.

"It's bullshit too," he subtly added. The group (primarily Christian-born yet lacking in belief) broke into nervous laughter, surprised by his bluntness.

A week prior, during our first full day in Delhi, I had asked Varun about one of the Hindu gods that we saw at the temple. He mumbled on about what the god is known for, and after his knowledgeable explanation, he half-jokingly said,

"It's bullshit."

Laughing, I reminded him, "Varun, you just said, 'bullshit' in a temple!"

He laughed with me, knowing the inappropriateness of his language—that is, if he really had believed any of it.

But I believe in Christianity, and although I do find it inappropriate to call my mythology bullshit, he doesn't, so, "Yeah," I replied, "you might be right." I could see why he would consider the miracle bullshit as many do consider it just that, but like the card game B.S. (Bullshit), every once in a while, someone is telling the truth, even if it sounds like bullshit, even if you couldn't comprehend it.

Emily was included in that group of nonbelievers, and still, we both found ourselves pouring our hearts out for the children in need. One evening, midway through our time in India, we sat on the edge of the porch overlooking the hand-worked fields skirted by the foot of the Himalayas. It smelled of smoke and the evening dew. Cows called out in the distance as we listened in between bouts of reflection. She felt her experience in India was not as transformational as she had hoped, I relented mine had been. India conjured questions about my future career and the lifestyle I was choosing to partake in. With these questions, I was not prepared to return to the home that was the source of my concern.

Earlier that day, I had watched our car speed by locals leisurely milling about their days which significantly contradicted the signs posted in the backroom of the retail store that might have become my permanent workplace declaring: "Speed is life." It was then I realized, I was part of that lifestyle. I worked fast to get more done to drive more sales to keep my job to keep my security in life. At the same time, I knew the Lord was my security and comfort. Maintaining that speed of life was just a rat-race that would take me nowhere but to these same thoughts—knowing there was more to life and wondering what I would do about it. My heart yearned for more. If it were feasible, I would stay at the two-story house off that winding dirt road forever with a cheery grin and a swollen heart. Pure joy filled out my unpainted eyelashes and tinted my cheeks; beauty surrounded and filled me. No resume could match the fullness of my soul. I wanted to abandon the world that awaited me.

The people we had the fortune of meeting and interacting with on the trip played a significant role in that internal conflict. When we visited McLeod, the home of the Dalai Lama, I spoke with a man whose dad owned a factory that produced scarves, and this son ran the shop. He studied sociology and was well-informed of the crisis in India—that local, brilliant people were exporting their work to support countries outside of its own. He was friendly and cheerful.

A shop just down the street had ornaments which were the souvenirs that my parents deemed most useful. I wanted to buy one for them as a gesture of gratitude and remembrance.

"One-hundred and fifty," the shopkeeper said approaching this display from another fold-up-shop he had been keeping watch on across the street.

"One-hundred," I bartered.

"No, I'm sorry I just can't do that," he responded. Not being very competent at negotiating, I agreed. As I was handing him the money, another man approached and introduced himself as the owner.

"What!? You don't even own these?!" I joked with the first guy.

"No, no, I just take the money." His smile was annoyingly endearing.

I turned to the owner: "How much?"

"One-fifty," he said.

"One-hundred!" I tried again.

"One-fifty."

"Okay, fine," I surrendered, and walked away with an ornament that surely got lost within the green needles of my parent's tree that next Christmas. Each person I encountered had an air of gentleness about them, a sense of joy.

After tutoring one afternoon, Ravi picked Connor and I up at the bottom of the steep, rocky hill that would take the wind out of me upon ascent. On our way back to the iSpiice house, we stopped at the two-room home of his brother's family. From the street, we walked to the back of the square, cemented hut and were greeted warmly by his sister-in-law and nephew. Ravi was different around them—less quirky and more manly; to my discomfort, he was unusually attractive. His nephew clearly loved Ravi, climbing all over his uncle and playing in a joking manner I couldn't understand. The woman offered us chai, and I played with his nephew who began jumping on the one bed their family shared.

He did somersaults, and we played peek-a-boo with a blanket. I was amazed at their beauty and generous hospitality.

I saw an attractive lifestyle there—a simple one, a sincere one, a joyful one. I compared it to what I knew from home and was frightened by the differences. I desired a peaceful life. One with flexibility, and simple joys. One with beautiful people and service to them. One with reasonable conveniences and opportunity to do great things. One that was suitable for a family. One that was pleasing to the Lord. My deepest desire is to be happy which comes by many ways; could it come from this place too?

Of course, this place was not exempt from suffering; our mere presence indicated that. In the girls' computer class that Sam and I taught in the mornings, Shipali, a student who was losing hearing due to a brain tumor, wrote us a note and asked us to work closely with her. Shipali was an eager learner who loved science and read frequently. I responded with a letter expressing our excitement to have her as a student and affirming her great potential. We did what we could to support this young girl who faced a challenge greater than most ever know. She put so much faith in us—even bringing her dad to class to meet us, a meeting that felt rather purposeless as we stood pushed apart by our language differences looking at one another, waiting for something consequential to happen. She was scheduled to have an operation on her tumor later that day; I could see the plea for help in his eyes. My helplessness matched his, and I still wonder if there truly wasn't anything I could do for them.

My heart grew for these people, though I was particularly fond of Ravi with his club foot, missing tooth, and all.

He slapped my thigh playfully with the backside of his hand that fluttered between the stick to the steering wheel. The warm winter wind of India moved gracefully through my air-dried hair, my face free from paint for weeks. Surveying the curvy fields that bordered the bottoms of the Himalaya Mountains, I smiled with a deep contented joy at Ravi's method of communication. I turned to him as he stared intently down the road as if nothing happened, and I thought I saw a smile hiding within him.

"What?" I asked with anticipation of what broken English words he'd spew this time.

"How are you?" he responded with greater emphasis and a higher pitch on the "you." Although I wasn't, I told him for the sake of simplicity,

"Good. How are you?" I couldn't easily sum up how I was feeling, or express it in the few sporadic English words he knew, or the few Hindu words I knew.

"I am good."

"Good," I affirmed with a smile, returning my stare down the road. I knew this moment was coming—my last drive to school down these winding roads through the small villages. Each village road was lined with three sided shops opening to the front and filled with cheap, expired snacks, local fruits and vegetables, or fabrics. He hit me again, bringing my attention back to him.

"I miss you and I love you," he said with an innocent smile that was comforting and sincere. I had yet to consider where my feelings began or stopped for these men who quickly but meaningfully became a part of my waking life. In that instant, the past three weeks were expressed through this gentle expression and his dimpled grin that was endearingly missing a front tooth.

"I love you too Ravi. I'll miss you so much!"

"Yah. Tomorrow you leave, and I here cry," he explained raising his left hand which formed a fist over his eye. He twisted it as he demonstrated his sadness. I replied with equal distress:

"I will be bawling!"

Turning away, I reveled in this moment. With much experience in beautiful happenings, I have learned how to recognize the experiences that are memorable and worthy of possessing forever. In recognizing them, I grasp and hold them tightly for as long as I can sense their warmth. With my head turned away from Ravi and towards the rolling hills and passersby leisurely making their way, I smiled. This is what I had come here for—to love and be loved.

About an hour later, Emily, Sam, and I sat in metal folding chairs along the left wall inside the principal's office. Our assistant Vineet, driver Ravi, and a few administrative men sat mirroring us on the other side of the narrow office decorated only with a thin coat of flaking paint. As we waited quietly in between awkward explanations in broken sentences from the principal, I glanced around the room intentionally, trying to find a comfortable place to set my stare. I met Ravi's stare. He sat directly across from me, with his legs crossed, more still than I had ever seen him before. For that moment, he existed innocently, without the fortune of movement or show, as he was—a man I came to know and love. I smiled at him, partly out of habit but mostly to alleviate discomfort by sharing in this moment. Ravi returned a bashful smile and diverted his glance quickly.

My experience in India was more than I could have dreamed. Every cultural encounter was humbling, purifying, and spiritual. My eyes saw the breadth of the human experience and feet tread its expanse. I looked deep into the heart of souls and saw nothing but goodness. The Lord is present in his people, and there is so much peace and joy to behold in the world, even in the unlikeliest of places.

———

I am lost. My shepherd is near, but I cannot decipher his direction.
Anxiety consumes the clouds above, and fear, the grass I tread.
Have my cries grown louder than his call?
For I cannot hear him, not at all.

Oh, how do I get home when these mountains I do not know?
The cliff, the slope, the bed, where must I rest my head?
Oh, Shepherd find me, for your staff I cannot see.

Another End

I clasped my mom's hand to my right, and my cousin Andrea's to the left. The others followed suit while gathering around Aunt Kim's bed.

"Who would like to lead?" After moments of silence, my mom prompted, "Claire?"

Gasping for air, I croaked "Dear Father," and cleared my congested throat.

Only an hour earlier, I had driven into the parking ramp searching through the snowfall and crowds of visitors for a place to park. My brother called suggesting I hurry to Kim's room because they were going to let her go soon.

"What do you mean?" I asked, confused as to why they would release Kim from the hospital so quickly after her stroke.

"They're going to take her off life support."

"Life-support!?" my voice broke as the severity of her stroke— untreatable because of her Leukemia—hit me, ran me over. I paused trying to catch my tears before responding. "...Okay." I wasn't prepared for any of this.

"Dear Father," I repeated, "Thank you for Kim's life. Thank you for the joy she shared with us and the love she poured out. We ask that you accept her into your heavenly home and that she lives in peace with you there. And we ask that you bring peace and comfort to those she leaves behind." She stirred in bed, her left arm rising, then falling, without purpose beneath the sheet. We paused as if expecting a certain resolution to our painful prayer but it was merely that, a silent pause.

"Amen," my mom concluded for us, signaling an "at ease" to our mourning stations.

Andrea and Mathias were numb. Eric was strong. Our family was dumbfounded. I watched the snow fall heavily through the window across the room—it was no unusual sight, possessing no meaning to this life-ending day, but I was uncomfortable to gaze anywhere else.

This beautiful woman, full of kindness and grace, laid helplessly on her deathbed, unrecognizable, some would wonder, to even God, as her dignity struggled within her to rise to the occasion and amass the graceful death she probably deserved. But alas, we are victims of this earth, and nature took another one.

I wondered whether someone who outwardly appeared less-than-interested in the path of Christianity would ever meet Christ and what He might say to her and if she would fall to her knees before Him. And how did she perceive the events leading to her rest? Would they possess significance in her new home? Where was that new home of hers?

Sometimes I wonder if we are too lukewarm to understand the gravity of our decisions here and now. For here and now pass quickly with little regard. But the Lord holds these thoughts and feelings and actions in great regard, for his love for us is too big to consider them less than they really are—either quiet acts of love or hurtful inconsideration. He longs for us our whole lives; he quietly waits for our "Hello," our "Yes," our "Amen." How great of an offense is our disregard for him, and how greatly he loves us in spite of it all. It's a great mystery, and an even greater gift, to be loved all the days of our life when even on our deathbed we fail to lift our eyes.

Convicted

I was in great distress. He had texted me in a sort of formality never seen or heard of before: "Do you want to have sex?"

Surprisingly, I responded, "Yes."

Thinking through my decision, I recounted my securities. I recalled I had a condom in my purse; just one. So, I grabbed it and kept it in safe keeping for the evening. As the day went on, I rethought my less-than-calculated decision. I recall a great sense of worry over what I would become if I did this. I regretted our agreement and the embarrassment of having to tell him I wouldn't have sex with him. The anxiety was too consuming; I needed to run to my father. Of course, this would be no casual conversation with my dad, so I tried to remain discreet in how I would tell him.

"I can't do it, Dad," I said bashfully, looking for my father's great love and validation of my feelings without disclosing what I was running from. I was seeking his protection. And in a loving but firm voice, he reminded me,

"You'll never be a great congresswoman if you can't communicate something like this to someone." I knew he was right and that I had to tell Kyle I wouldn't have sex with him.

I came to an elevator where I waited, perhaps having not even pressed the button. A mutual friend of Kyle's and mine joined me near the elevator. I confided in him too, praying someone else's wisdom might save me from this. But instead, he said this:

"Claire, someone someday will love and respect you so much." I didn't know what to say, so I said nothing at all. I stared down at the pavement waiting for the courage to arise within me. But I awoke.

I awoke with those same feelings of anxiety and heaviness. I realized my commitment to chastity ran deeper than a rule; it was a conviction, a truth I held within me. It was a truth that I knew would lead me to great love, and allow me to dwell in the greatest of love. For sex is an expression of love, a covenantal act that is the bodily union of the spiritual union established in marriage. It is meant to be selfless and fruitful, given without fear or constraint. No act of it outside of marriage can satisfy its purpose and its fullness. So, I wait for the fullness of love with bold confidence and joyfully pass on its poor substitutes.

Possibility

Returning from the Conservative Political Action Conference (CPAC) with the College Republicans, I was confident in the horizons I began to see. I remember walking into the large convention room in Maryland, filled with young persons in suits and dresses watching a panel discuss public policy. I remember being filled with a sense of purpose, and peace penetrated my soul. I felt I finally had found a suitable path.

It scared me. I didn't feel capable enough, strong enough, or wise enough for that path. I doubted myself. I was scared I was inadequate or unfit to become involved. But I couldn't see myself anywhere else. I had to encourage myself to run towards it, especially when I saw the Lord leading me.

I saw the path he set before me: how I began watching The West Wing that past January which sparked an interest in government, then took International Business Law which sparked an interest in law, then my friend Kathleen invited me to a College Republicans meeting where I first heard Tara Mack speak, for whom I became an intern, which solidified my attendance at CPAC with Representative Mack's Legislative Assistant, Rachel, who would get me a job on a local campaign that summer. The dots connected and the Lord was holding the pencil.

I can see you, Lord, in the way your Spirit moves me. You are forever faithful to your child.

Fear

I am terrified. I don't know what I am doing or what I want to be doing or with whom I want to be doing it. I have always dreamt of the day pursuers came running to the door but I never prepared myself to answer that door, for on the other side is a person I have put so much hope in.

Every time, I secretly hope he will not knock, that he will just sit at the door and eventually get bored and walk away. I expect to find irreconcilable faults in him as there have always been. I expect he will not possess the qualities I need in a partner. I look for reasons to turn the lights out and pretend I'm not home. But what I need is someone who won't leave because I'm not home. Someone who will tell me I am worth waiting for and he's worth having in my life. I need someone to stick to his guns—the very ones that will one day protect me from harm. I need someone to show me that although he's not perfect, he's exactly what I need. Because if he's not, he will inevitably walk away without looking back. And I, I will be consistently puzzled as to why I cannot meet anyone worth keeping. I will forget that I am on the inside of the door; yet, they are on the outside. I am the one keeping them out, even the ones who desperately want to know what is inside and know what this place is all about.

And when the interior is so beautifully constructed by a master builder, intentionally decorated, and meaningfully filled, it longs to be adored and lived in. The landlord that ought to occupy and care for his prize cannot even get past the sitters who wish to use the house for a night or two on their journey to nowhere blessed. Thus, the house sits empty while so many want to enter and adore. But the door will not budge, the windows will not open. As a window sticks from not being opened, so does my door. The longer it sits closed, the harder it is to open. I fear what is standing outside that door today, and tomorrow, and the next. For whoever it is, he might be or not be everything I expected. In both cases, I tremble.

Neil

"Okay, one minute each, give us a piece of advice that you learned in your experience in the non-profit industry," the moderator requested from the panel. The four sat facing the auditorium filled with students attempting to fulfill their Business 200 requirements for graduation.

"Why don't we start with you, Neil?"

The young post-grad I had been eyeing down for the past hour leaned forward in a not-so-eager manner, folded his hands together on the table and set them directly under the microphone. And in the same manner he had answered every question that bordered between humble and arrogant, he proceeded to respond to this last one,

"Don't take advice." A nervous chuckle waved through the auditorium seats at his slight comment. The irony built as Neil's pause lengthened. A slight smile brushed across his face; we hadn't yet learned he could smile. He continued,

"Seriously, don't take advice. Whenever someone gives you advice, they only know a piece of the story or situation. They only know a part of you. So, their opinion is not sufficient. Go and ask people about their story and their experiences and use that as a tool for assessing your own situation and dictating your actions. Do what you need to do. And if you don't trust yourself with that decision, then you need to take a serious look at yourself and work on yourself until you can trust yourself to make the right decision." His honesty sank in, and the other panelists wiggled in their seats hesitant to add to that. Naturally, I don't remember what they offered; I beat on with only Neil's words at my feet for I saw how all of our paths are different, and will be directed by various promptings and callings—we are to discern those voices and walk our path according to our own vocations, according to our own stories.

A L e s s o n

My interest in a boy drew me to the event hosted by College Republicans. The room was filled with upperclassmen alcoholics with a strong bent towards politics and its perks. We were celebrating Cam Winton who was elected to something and gave a speech about that something. In it, he recognized a classmate of mine who had worked closely with him on his race. She was a young female and he commented that "eighty percent of men will pursue a promotion without knowing anything about the position, only twenty percent of women will do the same." He commended Angie for taking on something she didn't know how to do and encouraged other women to do the same. We must not let something we have never done stop us from doing something we want to do. We must make a habit of approaching what we don't know instead of turning away from it in fear. We must run towards the unknown.

V o w

The path to holiness is a battlefield. Two steps forward, one step back. Distractions often prevail and weaken our defense. Our legs tire and our spirit crumbles. But my hope remains constant as the passing time. My eyes open to see a new day and to renew my vow for holiness. A vow, like the cornerstone or seed. An orienting vow, a battle cry for my Savior's army, for my Savior who will come again without the time in our hearts. And so, we must live as if that time is indeed marked on our hearts, as if that time was tomorrow.

Lord, I renew my vow to your most holy will. I have been caught up in your love because of your vow to me. It is time that I return to you reverently and assuredly. For you are the King. I've given my life to you, oh Lord. I want you to use me as your servant. Direct me according to your will. Enable me on that path. And be with me, Lord, so I may walk with you and worship you in my heart always. For with you all things are possible; with you, I can love in return.

A Better Love

I waited so long to be cherished. I waited to be really, truly seen and earnestly heard. My heart longed, love-lonely. No whispers passed through my ears or breeze of laughter through my hair. My heart sat silent. Such tales of rhythmic heartbeats and breathlessness and heartspeak fell cold on my lips for I knew not how they heat the soul. I so desired to be on fire!

As I waited, I realized I could not wait in stillness. For while no man eagerly longed to hear my heart, oh how my God pursued me. Oh, how his love perfectly filled me, and his care wholly encompassed me. He whispered ceaselessly; he was the wind. My heart grew stronger as I received the great love he offered me. Truly, I became complete. No love was greater or more assured. He stirred me to laughter and overwhelmed me to tears. His gifts left me breathless, no longer was I restless. He set my heart afire!

I Thought it was Over

He still secretly controlled me. When he made a wake, I felt a typhoon. I discovered through social media one day that Cole would be at the Wild hockey game in St. Paul. My heart leaped with possibilities that he would reach out to me while he was in my neck of the woods. In my fantasy, he would drop by and proclaim his apologies for being an idiot, for being weak, and for being foolish. I wouldn't accept him back immediately, but demand that he fights for me. Because after all, I deserved better than his convenient appearances and half-hearted promises.

Nay, I deserved better than these fantasies.

My heart breaks recollecting the times he expressed his affection for me—the love I glimpsed only too slightly that I began to believe it might not have been real. It was unfair. It was not right. And two years later, I still wished something bad upon them. My subconscious would not let me hide my dark secret I must confess, for I even dreamed of their destruction. Oh, how love destroys my ability to love.

And yet, I tried to save myself by recognizing his fault in all of this and his dying love for me. But I still insisted on clenching the love he once showed me. Perhaps I was but a mere orphan of love, savoring every small bit of feed man threw my way. Perhaps I staked my definition of love into the land on which we roamed even though it became barren and I simply existed to wait for him to return from a war he was too cowardly to wage. I awaited his return daily. My heart only accepted the hopefulness of his victory while it shuddered from the possibility he could not return or worse, would not return.

I pray that another will come and uproot my definition of love and deracinate my bearings on life. I must believe someone is willing enough and powerful enough to accomplish such a feat. For if not, I risk a hardened heart that softens only to harden again by the same.

Chapter Four

Examination

WILLMAR

I graduated from college on a Saturday and three days later I met my new colleagues at the Kelly Inn hotel conference room down the street from the Capitol. We reviewed the Campaign Handbook that covered budgeting, campaign committees, marketing, parades, signage, and every piece of campaigning usually overlooked by candidates. I was overwhelmed, both by the breadth and height of the work I was taking on. Hours earlier, I had submitted my final marketing project for my undergraduate degree which included marketing strategies for radio, direct mail, and newspapers, and my new job, to my surprise, was asking this of me too. Though, those duties were secondary to doorknocking—something I became all too familiar with the succeeding *years* to come.

The first week, we practiced doorknocking together in nearby districts handing out session wrap-ups from Republican Caucus Representatives and reminding people there would be a midterm election that fall. The days were tiring, proving my body's unfamiliarity with extended periods of (or any) exercise. The morning after my first five hours of doorknocking it took me three times as along to make it to the bottom of the staircase; I wondered if I could physically even make it through another day. I had two Advil capsules for breakfast and tucked my dread for the day into my sneakers before putting them on. Doorknocking was not hard—it was good exercise, gave me time to think about conversations I planned to have or about interview responses for when I'm on *Live with Kelly* someday, and allotted me some engaging conversations. But the tediousness of doing it for hours on end, every day, began to wear on me. But every day, I tucked it into my shoes and kept on moving.

Meanwhile, I eagerly waited to receive my assignment for the summer. Not only would the assignment dictate who I would be working closely with, but also where I would be working—I could be sent anywhere in Minnesota, some would say even to "no-where" Minnesota.

"Where?" I asked Rachel, my intern-manager-turned-boss, on the other end of the phone.

"Willmar," she reiterated and described the small-town's direction and distance from the cities, an area I couldn't picture having never been that way before. She assured me I was one of the lucky ones considering my candidate, Dave Baker: a small business owner who was the President-Elect for the Minnesota Chamber of Commerce and a community hero. I had expected to head two hours south to Rochester instead of two hours west, but I trusted that God's plan was a better plan.

I had no idea what he was expecting out of his staffer; I'm sure he didn't know what to expect of me either. We were both new to this. I paced back and forth in my parent's living room staring at the number on the notepad on the floor. I had rehearsed in my head what I would say and what information I needed to get from him. This would be the man I'd work with for the next six months; I had to make a good first impression. I mustered up the courage to call. The summation of what I needed to know about Dave came in our first telephone conversation:

"Claire! I'm so excited to have you on the team!" His excitement encouraged me. His humility inspired me. His friendliness welcomed me.

So, I made my first trip out to Willmar—a two-hour drive straight west from the Twin Cities. I packed an overnight bag after Dave offered to put me up in his Super 8 hotel so I didn't have to drive back to the cities that night. I met Dave at the Chamber of Commerce where his executive team had their regularly scheduled meetings. He sat across from me, reclined with one arm extended casually on top of the table. He gave a well-rehearsed summary of his life up to that point, and I, keeping a proper posture, briefly added my relevant work experience, which worried even me when my description ended in fifteen seconds.

Ken entered with his three-inch binder filled with campaign schedules, lists, and documents and sat at the head of the table, his long legs stretching out from underneath. He was a very tall man with a firm demeanor—which I later learned did not do justice to his sweetness. Ken was Dave's long-time best friend. He was the President of the Chamber of Commerce and fellow Republican who was a constant stream of support for Dave in his various endeavors. Ken was organized and strategic and straightforward when Dave needed it. Terry came in next. He was shorter with a thick, dark beard that concealed his age. Perhaps it was his rosy cheeks that made him appear so jolly, but his hearty laugh affirmed it. Terry was our tech-guy. Phil was the last one I met, and perhaps my favorite. He was in his late twenties with a boyish look to him. He was smart and creative with a sharp sense of humor and a half smile that could melt your heart.

As a field staffer, I was present to fill in the blanks and act as a liaison between the House Republican Caucus (HRCC) and Dave's campaign. Dave was in charge of his campaign, but the HRCC wanted to have their input heard, and used. The team wasn't quite sure what that would look like, nor did I. But we ran with our resources and began drafting a plan to bring us a victory on election night. The initial meeting was awkward with no clear takeaway except the confirmation that I had no idea what I was doing which Dave himself picked up on:

"So they gave me a newbie!" he said.

After the introductory meeting that left me with more questions and more work, Terry and I chatted about this and that and exchanged phone numbers. His wife was playing in a volleyball league that summer and Terry thought I might like to come to their game that night. I left the Chamber and checked into the Super 8, changed my clothes, and headed out to the old, and nearly abandoned, Kandi Recreation Center only a few minutes away. It was a sad excuse for a recreation center, but as a big city girl, I didn't expect much of Willmar. The wooden porch that rested between the bowling alley and the volleyball courts was crowded with mid-thirties volleyball fans splitting pitchers of beers and enjoying the start to summer. Nervously, I scouted out the place in my pale blue joggers that were a bit fashion-forward for the t-shirt-loving crowd and found Terry sitting at a table with a few friends. I sat down, and Terry poured me a cup. His wife Janice was a sweetheart with a deep, nasally voice. We chatted about her work and her life with Terry, and she asked about my job. Throughout the course of the summer when I would answer that very same question, I found that nobody really seemed to get it, but everyone appeared to be amazed that I agreed to whatever it was I was doing. Most young people moved away from that town, not to it. And I'd always agree with them and wonder why I ever agreed to it myself. Not that it was a bad job, but one of the strangest—moving to a rural community to doorknock and run a local political campaign after college. People would often refer to it as an internship, though I was never offended by that demotion. We shared some laughs and didn't keep track of the score, and I went home with a full heart and great excitement for what the rest of the summer would hold.

I stayed at the Super 8 for four days, which was then thought of as an indefinite amount of time. Dave had been looking relentlessly for a comfortable place for me to stay; he was hoping to find me a place on the lake where I could have my own retreat after a long day at the doors, but sure enough, my greatest retreat was the Tengwall's.

Dave called me with great excitement and the name of a family who said they might have a place for me. From the initial conversation, it sounded like they had a small apartment available for me near a lake, which was technically true but not as I had expected. Dave gave me Tom's number, and I blindly called this stranger to see if they would offer up their home. Tom was chipper on the phone, delightfully energetic and immediately mentioned a commonality—their son was a St. Thomas graduate as well. He invited me to come check out the place that evening, so, although I let him give me directions which meant nothing to this newbie in town, I plugged the address into the navigation on my phone and took off north towards the next town, Spicer, to meet "Coke and Tom." I drove down the road that wrapped back into the woods and came to the base of a hill. A long driveway led me up towards their house that sat surrounded by lush trees and flowers. A woman I believed to be Coke stood at the edge of their landscaping welcoming me with a broad smile and genuine, dramatic wave. She then directed me to a suitable parking spot in the driveway and came to greet me with a hug.

We hit it off immediately. Tom offered me a vodka lemonade on the warm summer evening, and we sat around the kitchen bar talking about anything under the sun that helps one get to know another. Eventually, Tom took me on the grand tour that led me from the upstairs to the main level to the semi-completed basement. "No pressure," he said as he waited for me to state my decision on whether to stay with them or not. It was not the separate apartment that I was looking forward to, and I had only just met these people, but I had no other offers, and it didn't seem like a bad option.

Without confidence I was making the right decision, I said,

"Sure," and he said,

"Okay, well, how long do you need to pack?"

That was really fast, but why bother waiting, I supposed. So, I drove back to the Super 8, packed my things that began to find their permanent places in the dresser and on the table tops of the hotel room, checked out, and headed back toward Spicer. Oddly, I was given my former classmate's old bedroom that was cluttered with basketball photos and awards. His clothes still filled the drawers and closet. Coke sat with me on the green carpet in his bedroom as she made room for some of my things and unfolded details about her family, especially our semi-common connection, their son, Erik, and we talked about how crazy all of it was. Coke quickly became a second mom, and Tom, a suitable dad. They would welcome me home after a sweaty day of doorknocking waiting to hear all the details of the day, often in amazement that this was actually someone's job. They commented on what they heard about the campaign and offered their perspectives and experiences. They were a refuge after a long day. They were spectacular, offering their humor—Coke with her anecdotes about people I had met and Tom with his razzing as a homegrown Democrat and feather-ruffler. Tom had invited a friend over one evening to watch a game and have a beer—I always excited to see new cars in their driveway when I came home, interested in meeting more of their family or friends. Tom, in his long, drawn-out way of setting up a story as I would hang onto every word preparing myself for another joke or dry piece of sarcasm that I might not otherwise catch, introduced me and my work to his friend. Tom then added that his friend was Mary Sawatsky's (Dave Baker's opponent's) cousin. I was not prepared for that interaction—my eyes widened and I hoped a smile was drawn out across my face. I struggled for a sensible word order to comprise a sentence to comment, but Tom was impatient and began laughing. His friend joined in. I stood uncomfortably, forcing a smile to alleviate my lack of participation in this fun they were having at my expense. Tom clarified,

"He's not her cousin. He's probably the most Republican person I know!" I laughed it off with his friend,

"You guys scared me!"

His friend proceeded to tell me how deeply conservative he was—probably, in my assessment, too conservative to believe that Dave was an adequate Republican candidate. We laughed it off and bonded over conservative qualms and passions. Though I didn't appreciate the humor of the prank as much as Tom, I reveled in the place I was and the people I was meeting. Coke and Tom were not shy about introducing me to their [fifty-year-old] friends and I quickly became everyone's adopted daughter or potential daughter-in-law.

As my peers asked about life in Willmar, I realized how strange it was to be living with parents at that point in my life, but it was the best thing for me. They were more inquisitive than friends and less annoying with parental inquisitions than my own parents—this had little to do with who my parents are and more to do with the fact that my parents were my parents, a largely universal sentiment I still struggle to understand. We spent Friday nights watching movies or sitting on their front patio with Coronas and limes next to the radio as we listened to the local high school football game (though I was usually just there for the company with my laptop in front of me working on voter targeting or direct mail drafts). If I wasn't with them, I was somewhere partying with the Bakers.

The Bakers, too, took me in as another daughter; I am eternally grateful for the way they planted me into their community. I was overwhelmed by their hospitality. They are kind, compassionate, generous, thoughtful, and welcoming. Even their friends had gone to great lengths to find me a home and make my new town a special place.

I loved what I was doing. I had to remind myself often to step back from the daily grind and admire it. I don't know why the Lord sends me where he does, but I am surely grateful for it.

Yet, I was there for work, and we worked hard. For six months, we pounded the pavement or grazed the gravel between five to seven days a week. Our hearts were heavily invested in the effort we employed. I suppose it was like an internship in that one day I nearly cried—I found myself doorknocking my opponent (I didn't look at the name close enough to catch the error on my walk list and approached her house in ignorance). Shock struck her face, and confusion overcame mine. As she took Dave's promotional literature from my hand, we had a brief, tense conversation—she scolded Dave on a trivial matter, and I smiled nodding my head during her lecture. I practically ran down her driveway with a target on my back and fought off stress-tears from my unfortunate encounter.

On our way back to Willmar after a long day of doorknocking towards the end of the race, Dave and I were reflecting on all things possible and all things past. He expressed his excitement, nervousness, fear, confidence, and peace. He talked about the great moments of the campaign and those to come when he would take office. He grabbed my hand across the center console that trapped cheese curds in its crevasses—we had spent two months in that truck hitting every door among corn fields and lakes—and proceeded to instill his confidence in me as a person, and particularly in my ability to find great love. Those feelings were already made evident by his comments when we'd approach a house with mini-four-wheelers in the yard, chickens running around, and toys scattered about, that that would be me with four kids and a handy husband. I liked that vision he had. And as we drove, with his hand in mine as if trying to transfer his care to me, he poured out his affection and my heart swelled. Our relationship was quite appropriately platonic, and a friendship I will forever count myself grateful for. I give him all the credit for that. His kindness and interest in the people and things in my life that weren't related to the campaign built a connection between us that likely no other candidate created with his or her staffer. And he was seemingly fully transparent with the pieces of his own life—sharing in the loss of his son, family struggles, the pendulum of friendships. His wife, Mary, was just as open about these same things. They are a tender couple with a history of great loss and a record of mighty love and triumph. I imagine if I portrayed a different personality, they might be less open. I like to think I'm easy to talk to and a good listener, but I give them all the credit for trusting me and for being honest about their past and present. Perhaps it was a case of small town personality—passing along the drama of their lives. But whether it's a commendable trait, or just what it was, they are truly two of the greatest people I know. And as a team, they've won many battles, including the 2014 District 17B race for State Representative, when Dave Baker became *State Representative* Dave Baker.

I awoke that next morning, Wednesday, November 5, in a haze—it could have been the alcohol that was trying to work its way through my system or the feat that had just been accomplished. I gathered with the Bakers around the breakfast table, the room still soaking in the glory (and disappointment) of a half-percent margin of victory. We could only marvel at it for so long; I left an hour later to gather the life I established in Willmar and to load it into my car. My exit felt swift and strange. Driving home with the dirt still caught in my car's interior from the hundreds of miles of backroads and with clothes piled above my rearview line of vision, I gazed ahead in wonderment of the past six months. That was the coolest thing I had ever done. But this new life I had assumed was being left behind for the next one; I was on my way to the House of Representatives to see where this path would take me, confident the Lord was still right there next to me.

His Hand

My journey is a constant surprise and a joy I never deserve. I am regularly amazed by Christ's guiding hand. Each step is filled with greatness and humility, love and hope. Fear is diminished by the presence of the Lord's healing hand. He renews me every day and sends me on my way. Even when I choose not to recognize him next to me, he is there loving me and wishing me well. And while his peace is overwhelming, it often goes unaccepted because of my humanity and friendliness towards this world which draws me deeper into its arms. But he never gives up on me.

CONSPIRACIES

It came up in conversation casually—well, as casual as conspiracies can be. The topic always somehow sneaks into a moment, where I, trying to be cute and smart and a bit unorthodox, call to mind the conversation topic's relation to a wildly proclaimed conspiracy theory. I would enthusiastically explain the idea without admitting my own belief in it. And they would shrug the idea off or challenge my position.

At a fundraiser for Dave Baker in Minnetonka that summer, Mike, Terry, and I knew no one but ourselves, so we gravitated towards making random conversation with one another, during which I learned from Mike how to sell Christmas trees—the line "I was saving this one for my mom but...." works nine out of ten times—and that Terry was trying to figure out how to identify the gender of a chicken by placing a sticker on the eggshell. And they learned that I am an avid conspiracy theorist. Mike questioned me on which theories topped my list and why. After getting carried away in my evidence I stole from documentaries and citizen bloggers, Terry chimed in.

"I totally get where you're coming from, but I've grown out of it," he said after I stopped myself from becoming too obnoxious. I couldn't tell if I should be grateful he understood my position or offended that he believed my position was something I would soon grow out of. In either case, I disregarded his comment, and we all moved on to bigger and better topics.

On the car ride home, I was feeling a bit tipsy and tired and had no idea how anyone else was doing, but again—half-heartedly—interjected a conspiracy theory that was related to the conversation. The gentlemen broke into song and dance again, questioning my stance. Terry repeated how he knew exactly what I was talking about but got past it. I asked him to clarify what he meant.

"I just realized that analyzing and worrying about it does nothing. My perspective of life is much bigger than human reality. God is the one who controls all of this anyway."

Of course, I knew he was right.

"Yeah, I know God is still bigger than all of this, but you can't just deny it's not happening. It is, and just because I believe it doesn't mean I'm denying God."

"Yeah, but you become obsessive when you should be contemplating greater things. Again, the root of everything is pride and selfishness."

"How does that relate to this?"

"Because you come to obsess—"

"—Oh my gosh, you're right. I'm proud to know their agenda! I find pleasure in knowing more and think I'm smart because of it. But, I will argue that it doesn't mean you have to disregard what's going on. I've never lost faith in God. I grew deeper in faith."

"Yeah, well it's not worth obsessing over."

I realized I needed to take a step back. As Sai Baba once said, "You seek too much information and not enough transformation" (okay, I don't even know who that is, I saw it on Facebook that same night, but I liked it, and the coincidence made me think God was trying to tell me something). I had been seeking more knowledge about worldly events that do nothing but tie me closer to earthly things that mean nothing of importance to my soul, my redemption, and my sanctification. God was definitely getting his message across. At the bookstore when I went to purchase a text on the fall of the US dollar, and ultimately the world economy, I stood in front of the current events shelf, enthralled. Whereas just a few years prior, I would have done the same in front of the Religion shelf on the other side of the room. My prideful desire to become more led me to an aisle that didn't know fulfillment.

"I believe God is in control of everything. Every day I wonder why I met who I did," Terry added. Well, I know why I met Terry.

THE JOURNEY

We caught up on her new, big-girl insurance job with Arthur Gallagher and my toils and pleasures of my first job out of college. She sat with a plastic knife in hand, cutting another small slice of chocolate fudge which would soon lead to another one. I went on to express my fears of changing jobs again that fall after the election. After my conversation with Terry, I feared this new pursuit in politics was a track that sent me further from my goals of living a holy life.

"I'm afraid this isn't a proper career for a good life. I could be working for a non-profit or become a nun. I think there's value in having a passion, it has to be in my heart for a reason, but because of it, I'm seeking consolation in earthly matters. Honestly, what do you think?"

She smiled, "It's funny you bring this up because this is exactly what I went through a few months ago. The reason I was taking so many interviews with different insurance companies and NET Ministries was that I was trying to find something meaningful. And I struggled with this because of my Catholic Studies classmates. Many of them had this mindset that the only good careers were becoming a mom, teaching, or working in some Catholic organization. But the thing is, though we are not of this world, we are in it. It operates by the collaboration of laborers and thinkers, blue collar and white collar. And Jesus needs us in there too. A career can be equally, if not more, holy outside of the four walls of a church if done with the right intention and in the right ways."

She affirmed our roles in the secular world could still contribute to building the Kingdom of God. So, these secular responsibilities may be harder for the soul to endure, but their challenges will be used to strengthen holiness in ourselves and others. Christians are not of this world, but we're needed in it.

OUTBURSTS

I couldn't live in the same world as him. Every action was too hard and too toxic. So, I ran to my phone to type a text message:

The way you treat me is not okay. Lately, you always seem to be cutting me down for a laugh, and while it usually produces one, I'm not laughing anymore. The way you become aggressive towards me is not fair, warranted, or respectful. The brass conversations you rarely hold with me are pointless. To think you treat me (and even our mom) with such aggression and unkindness disgusts me as your sister. If you persist in treating me without kindness or respect, don't ever think you can count on me as your ally or friend. You may be my brother, but I don't need you, and you don't need me. So figure it out or don't. I'm washing my hands of this.

As much as I desired to hit the send button, I wondered: What if this was the last thing I said to him? Do I really mean this? Do I need to say it? As my friend Courtney would have advised, I decided to wait twenty-four hours.

I waited twenty-four hours. And rightfully or not, I still wanted to say what I had to say. Yet, again, I withheld because the more I thought about what I wanted to say to him, I realized what I really wanted to do was hurt him and restore justice for what he did. I wanted to threaten him; I wanted to make him feel bad about himself as I thought he should. Saint Pope John Paul II said it best: "It is better to cry than to be angry because anger hurts others while tears flow silently through the soul and cleanse the heart." As I practiced what I would say to him in person the following weekend during my visit home, I began to cry thinking about what he did and how much I wished things were different. As I cried, I recalled that quotation, understanding I should not act in anger towards Alex because, whether or not I believed he deserved such brashness, I am not the final judge who is authorized to deploy such justice; I am the one who is called to love my brother no matter what. If I were to say everything I felt, I would be a mere pawn of the devil who seeks the destruction of souls. I would not let anger hurt others, only my afflicted self. The gate is narrow, and I was not willing to sacrifice eternity for a few minutes of improper justice, even though I certainly had in the past.

So, I tried to mend. He was reckless with my offering of reconciliation. Perhaps I approached him all wrong. He sat across from me, at the dinner table to which I had invited him. My intentions were good, and his might have been only for a free meal at our favorite local restaurant, but if they were otherwise, they were kept behind his perpetual facade. We used to do this often during our college years, but while he got lost and wandered painfully in those days, so did our friendship. My little brother was volatile, and I continued moving forward while he was moving in a different direction, thus separating us from one another. I could hardly understand this reasoning—I felt vain asserting his anger stemmed from jealousy or insecurity as much as my parents may have offered me that resolution. Perhaps it had nothing to do with his feelings towards me. Perhaps it was the effect of sadness or the blank canvas before him that taunted him to the point of insanity. Though, maybe it did stem from a lifetime of hatred towards me that I had never seen boiling beneath his skin.

Whatever the case might have been, I knew it was strong enough to become physical. He had hit me with a force as shocking as a dirty word in your fourth-grade classroom. Playful hits and kicks were a pass-time for my brothers, dad, and me. This particular time, my dad sneakily moved towards Philip and I—a motion I knew too well after twenty-two years. Philip reacted first, hitting Dad on the bicep. I rang in with a playful blow to Dad's back. For the next minute, Philip and I exchanged action-movie quality moves, and Alex joined in. Naturally, I hit back—again, playfully. Alex's demeanor quickly transformed without warning. He kicked back hard with a face I had become too familiar with. He mumbled something offensive, and I tried to strike back. One thing led to another, and my dad came in between us. I commented on Alex's inability to play, and he slapped me across the back of the head with the intention to hurt.

We didn't talk for months.

Still, there I sat at that restaurant, in disgust, watching him eat his loaded mashed potatoes. I had offered him an alternative: faith. What I desired for my brother were happiness and peace. I know that comes from Christ and sought to offer it to him as an alternative to the way he was carrying his burdens. He chewed it to pieces, spit it out, stomped on it, and laughed. My heart broke. That he might see the faith—our Savior, the one person who was fighting for him and died for his sake—as nothing more than pathetic, brought me to tears. Alex's one good chance at finding true peace was disgusting to him. To see a soul turn away from Christ with such disdain wrenched my heart. And then his words against me tore it apart. Again, when we departed ways, I left a trail of tears.

I waited in prayer. To my parents' dismay, I lacked interest in a relationship with Alex as I knew him. I had tried, but too many times I had been turned away with a disdainful comment or hostile word. I could not control how he perceived me, and frankly, I don't care how he does, he is no proper judge. What I care for is peace, and I cannot create it alone. So, I stand alone, waiting for him to come around. Philip did. Alex will too.

But then a year later, I answered my mom's call. She spoke slowly and discernibly as I sat impatiently on the phone once again. She explained the next episode of Alex's. As her story unfolded, I sat silently, for all the words had been exhausted by stories like this before. My heart quieted and my soul bled. I let it drip in rhythm with hers. Both compassion and impatience pooled in my eyes, for I understood the personal power of thought and equally recognized the art of temperaments. Thus, I was at a loss for resolution and my commentary—muted.

A week later, I would find words sufficient enough for comment. My mom had elaborated on her interactions with Alex since his knuckles bled at the mercy of a door, relenting that he compared himself with others and was too hard on himself. In that image of him, I saw a reflection of myself and, likely, everyone I know. She unfolded the reasons, the excuses, the pains and I cautioned against using his liberal diagnosis. Though some people are focused enough to evade the game of comparison, many fend it off daily. I heard these seemingly natural battles of his, recognizing them in my own life, and suggested we differentiate between being sad and being depressed (as we know it today). I imagine when we accept that we are depressed, we fold ourselves into the diagnosis, accepting assumed limitations and timelines and thinking to ourselves that there is no way out but through the traditions of drugs and therapists and victimhood. Rather, if we are to see our state as a place of sadness, knowing that with appropriate discernment and clear intentions we can move from this place to the next without the crutch of drugs, we can move more healthfully toward peace.

I fear that by the powers and interests of our healthcare industry, we have become pawns in their corporate games. The doctors, earnest for their patients' recovery, I do not blame. For nutrition classes that reveal the critical and helpful effects of our food are left as electives, if offered at all, and drugs are introduced as the quickest remedy for patient care and that the adverse side effects are simply the price paid for "getting better." But when I see a commercial for a prescription drug that should be used with an antidepressant if the antidepressant is not alleviating all the symptoms, I am struck with disdain for this culture. Meanwhile, I sat on the other side of that screen battling my own anxiety of where I was and where was going in this world. Only an hour earlier was I in that car with my parents explaining how Alex's feelings were surprisingly similar to many of mine that I battle daily. I was not depressed. No, I was learning what was important to me; I was learning how I must grade myself when no one did it for me; I was learning about value and work and meaning.

This—being a single, twenty-something in the early 2000s—is the most challenging time in my life. No longer do teachers and parents award me for my character, no more do they praise me for my aptitude or recognize my merits or the person I am becoming. Every four months now I am not given a new start with new classes and new teachers and new projects. Every year there is not another calculated level to surpass. Society has not laid before me the course of the next four years. So, I sit at my dining room table crowded with my materials for taxes, a day's to-do list, and thank you cards I need to mail, and I fret over the minutes that are passing. I don't have a plan for the next minutes or days or years to come. A career is not boiling beneath my skin and the assurance that I'm doing okay is not written in red pen and hanging on my fridge. I am faced with years that are as dark and barren as the depths of the ocean, and sometimes I feel like I'm drowning in them. I don't know if I've trained well enough to get me to the tomorrow I should be chasing. The option of school is always before me, but I do not know if I should go back, what I would go back for, and where I should go. Though if I stay out of school, do I stay in politics—is there a career there, is it the best course—or do I work towards marketing or my passions? What even are my passions? The questions are greater than the strength I bear to discover the answers. My best friends are a day away from engagements with incredible men, and I remain single and unsure of whether the sisterhood is a better fit for me anyway. I am weighed down by the options before me. I am unquestionably blessed to be able to ask these questions and have these options. Oh, how blessed I am. Much will be asked of those who have much. So, I wait, listening in earnest—but likely not in best practice—for the demands of my Father who I so desperately want to serve. I trust that God has called me here, in my despair, to the wood of my table to pour out these doubts, these pains, these agitations of this earthly life, to discover his presence within me and to see how he smiles with compassion on his child who is so weary and anguished over nothing. Our Lord is good; he is too good for what I deserve. Though I feel his silence, and his silence brews a storm within me, I wait for it to settle knowing the Lord is approaching. He has never led me astray. He loves me tenderly; he loves me right out of my darkness.

Though we stand on different blocks in our journeys, the fears, the doubts, and the confusion, I believe, are much the same and equally crippling. So, I commiserate with my distant brother and beg he takes the hand of our Lord who extends it with compassion.

WAITING

It's the exhilarating idea that around every corner, I might fall in love—head over heels, soul-finds-mate kind of love. Without that potential, corners have little meaning and doors have little hope. I awaken with the chance that I might fall deep into someone's world that day and get lost in a paradise of acceptance and admiration even the earth's bounty cannot satisfy. My name becomes a spell and his, the most my heart can whisper.

MORAL GUIDES

We are masters of our own reality. We are righteous in our compassionate actions. We are judges of our own fate. This is the thinking of my generation which will blight the next, and entrap their next, without their ever discovering.

This generation seeks the affirmation of their corruptible hearts on which they base their morality. To them, inherent truths are fleeting, and the movement of the times is their sound reasoning for action. Problems are bandaged with disoriented means. Judgment is based on their perception of reality. And so, through these false authorities of life, gods are made daily within themselves.

This idea was first made aware to me by a close friend freshman year of college who had recently fallen away from the Church. She explained one of the reasons she didn't stand by the faith was because she didn't think it was right just to accept what the Church teaches without thought of one's own. She, like many, thought she could pick and choose what was true or not. She denounced the moral guide the Church is meant to function as and favored one's own discovery and model of the truth. When she first explained this, I felt she perceived my source for truth as foolish because it came from some place other than myself. So, I felt foolish because, of course, it's reprehensible to adhere to a moral code you yourself did not create. So, since then I have felt the need to justify, from my own knowledge and wisdom, why something was right or wrong because a simple "because the Church teaches that" would not and should not suffice. She was telling me it was wrong to have a rock on which I stand.

Now I do believe it is important to understand why the Church has arrived at its teachings, but should we ever consider it foolish to support something because we are well-justified in supporting it and everything that follows from it? No.

We are made fools because we have a guiding moral code and source of truth. The world laughs as each takes their throne in their own hearts. My peers and those alike have heightened themselves and every other human to a god wherein he or she can create his or her own moral standard or identity and no one should be told differently. Now as a product of this generation I largely have, unrightfully, agreed with that—although I have my own beliefs, who am I to say whether something is right or wrong for someone else, especially when considering the government's role in it all.

But the problem is, there are an inherent morality and truth that our society rejects, and this rejection is being normalized, and its nonconformists degraded and ostracized. Their warfare is brilliant.

By turning the morality on the moral, on what do the moral have to stand? Abortion is for the welfare of women, homosexuality is a matter of human rights, and forced religious observation of their progressive laws supports religious freedom. Any grounded argument is being beaten and bruised, pounded by the wave of culture and those that have chosen to ride it. Their succeeding generations will drown in the folds of this wave, and there will be no land on which to stand.

But we are not masters of our own reality. We are not always righteous in these compassionate actions. We are not judges of our own fate. We need to realize this before it's too late and we find ourselves miserable only to wonder how we've become this disordered and how we can continue to fill this void that our hearts have longed for since our inception. When we see this, only then will our walls fall and our hatred cease. Only then can we begin to restore our human condition and bring forth all the beauty and grace that flows from it.

CLOSURE

I always knew I needed it. It was just a matter of getting it. The challenge of achieving it seemed unsurmountable but crucial. For three years, I had avoided all conversations of past relationships (not that there had been many inquiries from curious subjects). If I allowed myself to advance to a second or third date, that conversation would be had, and I'd be left staring into the bruises of my heart and getting lost in their mystery. If I could not understand what I experienced first-hand, how could I begin to explain it to a stranger? Those years of torture, which I often buried as love, were not capable of being sufficiently labeled without the help of their co-conspirator, Cole.

At a professional soccer game, Kathleen rambled about surely something significant and Ryan, viewing the game a bleacher seat behind us, leaned in to listen. Drawing my gaze back to my fellow fans, I agreed with Kathleen wholeheartedly about the importance of getting closure. Ryan studied my face, noting my hesitation in continuing my comment, for which reason he did not know. But his hunch was close enough to hit my buttons, "Cole?"

Although I immediately resorted to playing defense, as I'd been so conditioned to do by the mention of his name and a presumed relationship by others, I admitted he was correct. I so badly wanted to share this part of my life with those who might understand or have sympathy for me, but I saved the drama for another time.

The conversation stuck with me. I began to think critically about the option of seeking closure. I craved it as much as water. My bruises still hurt. But returning to their father was as dangerous as walking away. On a walk with my friend, Emily, during that time of consideration, I sought her advice since she lived through every minute of it with me as my roommate freshman year. She merely responded with a question:

"Do you think he could be honest with you if you did ask whether he really loved you?"

The problem was seeking closure was almost as damaging as not having it. My ideal outcome was for him to sit across from me, tell me he saw a future and was crazy about me—to confirm I was not making it up. What I feared was he would either say that which was contrary to my belief: that he never really loved me romantically and was just having fun. Or worse, that he would avoid vulnerability and lie through his teeth behind which he was screaming, "I love you." Perhaps he was also lying to himself as a man who so desperately loved a woman but never accepted it into his belief system because of fear, or inconvenience, or whatever it was that was blinding to that man. I saw the latter as the most likely case, or did I hope it was the most likely case? I would never have a sufficient answer to solve the mystery of my past which haunts me to this day. My search for closure was as good as running into a beehive for apple juice.

But I couldn't just let the wind carry the pages of those years away; those pages were too important to let go of. So, I must resolve, on my own, in my own way, the nature of those years. I must keep a semblance of truth, a front of assurance, even if it may be wrong, for I must move on.

THE END OF THE WORLD

The angst of the unlived life has made heroes out of the dying and lions out of the living. It has brought adventure to the dormant and urgency to the slothful, teaching us not to concern ourselves with dying but what we might miss through it and because of it, thus calling humanity to a fuller life.

Yet, I sat at the cluttered kitchen counter with my mom—my life yet filled with all the accomplishments I find myself capable of or the adventures I continually dream up—and told her a reality only the hopeless dare to admit. That I, in partial unison with them, do not fear the unlived life, do not dare miss that which will go unlived, and do not wish for it more than death. Rather, I don't consider the unlived life anything but a mere conception of the disoriented. And today as in many times before, and unfortunately likely many times ahead, I have regressed to one of them.

I see the signs of the times and hear the conspiracies in the lies and fall disheartened. Many of the wise and the foolish have attested to the coming of Christ and the end of times. And although we cannot know the exact time when Christ will come again or perhaps when Russia will launch a nuclear attack or even when the artificially inflated financial system will finally crash, there will be signs warning us of its nearness. Don't bother wasting time searching for these signs yourself—any relevant internet search will populate 121 videos of Obama as the anti-christ or details of the looming financial collapse.

These days of personal torture—that is, searching for the signs which knowingly evoke great fear and paralysis—have come and gone cyclically for me, and ironically, or perhaps more so consequently, have arisen when my heart was furthest from Christ's. Fear would cripple me, and I would count all that I have not done and all that would go un-lived.

And the times when such signs only arise within me the hope of His promise, I have been closest to him. I told my mom,

"If I do not wake up tomorrow, I'm okay with that." I bled out cautiously in fear of offending the woman who partook in giving me that life. As tears swelled in both our eyes, I continued on, impassioned by the truth I had seen so clearly,

"I know that if I am to die today, I have lived a great life. I have done and seen incredible things. There's a lot more I could do and plan to do, but if I die, I am confident that I need not any of that because my time has come. And everything that has led up to that moment in time was for that moment and nothing more for my sake. My purpose is to earn my heavenly reward. That is where my happiness rests and if I can be there tomorrow, let it be. And if not, I have more to do here."

With these words resting heavily in the air like the impenetrable smoke of an addict, I awaited her projection of a pious, disingenuous little girl oblivious to the realities of life. Rather, she just sat there, listening. And I began to laugh. And we carried on to some other lines of conversation. And I will never forget the freeing feeling of knowing the truth—of being unchained from every course of life that is plotted and planned for us and every dream or desire ever set before us, leaving only one yearning: the one that will lead us to deliverance.

I can only recall that feeling; I do not possess it as of today. For in writing this, I regrettably am having trouble retrieving this same peace in death I experienced a few years back, such is my cause for writing this—to regain the sentiment on life the Holy Spirit once inspired. That peace that once controlled my thinking has been pushed out as I pulled the world back in. Perhaps, the urgency of living I now feel will propel me toward certain salvation or perhaps it will only further disorient me. In either case, having once discovered this truth, it can't go away but only speak to me that which I must be reminded of: I am here to live a good and holy life of love and sacrifice for the greater glory of God and in turn, to be welcomed into heaven on that final day. I must constantly recall that that is what my heart should be set on. Nothing I could dream for tomorrow could surmount the wealth in Christ's promise of everlasting life.

THESE TIMES

I feel it coming—the times that were spoken of long ago and shoved into a book that collects dust on the shelves within the hearts of the foolish. While movies of it were made for mere entertainment, sermons of it went unheard or misunderstood. So, we continue to anticipate the regular arrival of tomorrow with no prayer for our souls during the setting of its prequel. We must be ready, always, for the end of days, for the coming of our Lord, incessantly accepting its goodness and pushing away the things that would make us think otherwise.

———

Do not expect tomorrow, nor put faith in it—but rather in He who is the giver of the eternal tomorrow.

MY PAST

I sat in the back row, directly across from Sydney. She stood timidly behind a choir stand, her back to the sacristy and her eyes nervously pacing the pages set before her. She began a talk on the saint of the day with a shy reservation and an uncertain tone that transported me into a classroom on the day of project presentations. She reminded me of what I might have been like at that age, and what most of us probably were: sheepish, unconfident, and concerned about the opinions of our peers. While I recalled high school, my memories of accomplishments, doubts, and moments of pride and shame were invited too. As the years unfolded quickly within my mind, so did the layers that I was comprised of. The seats behind me became filled with the various stages of my growth into adulthood: the church Claire, the popular Claire, the athlete, the invisible, the musician, the politico, the wild, the manager, the solitary, the surrounded, the hopeful, the burdened, the very so confident Claire and the very so reserved. These versions that surrounded me felt like strangers, like the stranger that was once a dear friend, like the stranger you had once cherished so sweetly. And then, I absorbed them, into my skin, into my bones. It was all me. It is who I am.

Sitting in this thickness of my being, in awe of its magnitude, I returned my gaze to Sydney, who one day, too, may remember this version of herself. I hope she accepts herself as she was there before us and honors her development into the person she one day will become.

THE CHASE

The colors of the fall blend into winter and those of winter into spring. As with those, one becomes the other, and so do I, as my tomorrow becomes my yesterday without my timely discovery. So, my regularly explored days become nightmares as I try to chase time, pulling myself out of the hole I dug myself into. Time runs faster, and in my pursuit of it, the things around me which always were so important become blurry in my peripherals and I find myself frantic, trying to catch all of it while remaining on the heels of time. When tomorrow comes, I don't understand why I spent all night in struggle. Then the hastiness arises again, and I continue my chase. Time drains through my fingers as I watch it splatter to the ground with my tears of lost dreams and spit of shameful disgust. We are only getting older.

BOLD

Be bold. Fear not the passing day, only the passing life. Adventure into the interests of the mind and passions of the spirit for that is where you will serve the world best. Scorn the trenches of wealth that trap you in their foolish attainment of things, for they will not keep you company or love you back. They burn in fire. Perhaps you will be burned tomorrow; this only serves as purification for you to rebuild what you do and who you believe to be. Seek the challenge. Embrace the changes in the wind; fighting against it will only tire your feet. And love the wind and her companions—the sun, the trees, the stars—for they are alive and dependent on your stewardship. Be bold. Live outside the lines that wrongfully serve only has a handicap. Welcome the uncertainty of what you might find past them for great risk commands reward. Seek the lesser of things and the better of selves. Be kind to your mistaken self as you only knew what you knew and not what you did not. Do not break the promises of your youth or seize the formation of future ones. The days change our clothes but the years change our hearts—where your heart is not, you are not. And where it is, you live.

I would much rather see it live than perish without notice. For the health of our hearts and souls are the foundation on which we live. We must first seek their perfection, detesting the promises of this world which do not deliver good but take it. They take humanity out of humans and turn brothers and sisters into foes. Perhaps that which does give unto us is only revealed to those who first give themselves. They give their time, their energy, their love, and companionship. They give of their talents and their stories, and they give of their spirit. As we know from St. Francis, it is in giving that we receive, and it is in dying that we are born to eternal life. And after all, that is what we truly seek.

I believe in something greater than today. That within me, there exists a capacity for greatness not yet tested and tried. But I am confident it one day will be. For if we are earnest and humble in our pursuit of our vocation, I do not believe we can fail in doing it. We were created with particular talents and abilities; we were created with intention. Our uniqueness is purposeful, and thus our vocations meaningful and needed in this world. We may search in many places before filling our seat at the table, so we should not fret at not finding that seat earlier than we will. Consider this search a continual revelation of God's glory and power and consequently, of who you are and can be in him. It is the perpetual pilgrimage of life.

MEANING

I cannot recall the importance of living. Or the meaning or the purpose or the way to do it. But what I know for certain is the power in the day and the trees that move like the wind and the sun tell them to. I know the Creator who made it and the birds that obey him. I drive to work wondering what this is for. Why do we persist with meaningless endeavors when the universe is telling us to slow down and feel the blood pulse through our bodies? Oh, how we move through the drama of our being.

WAR

I stood in my boss's office alone, peering through the tears swelling hastily in my eyes onto the hazy spring setting of downtown St. Paul with my phone to my ear.

"How do I know if I have a brain tumor?" I asked my mom with the small bit of courage I mustered to realize those words to life. She assured me it was nothing after I explained how one of my feet would frequently catch on the ground as I stepped forward, compelling me to fret over my depreciating motor skills and its cause. Her reassurance meant very little in contrast to the movie reel I played myself of the succeeding months fighting brain cancer. And after that movie ended, I needed to know if it would remain on the shelf or in me.

Granted, though I have the urge to laugh as others do at my story, I could not dismiss my concern. Weeks earlier, as I arranged my pillows and tossed back-and-forth to find the sweet spot in which I would rest, my body was also doing things I hadn't told it to do. I laid there, feeling these motions roll through my limbs and excite my heart. For nights, this went on around the same stroke of midnight. After bringing this to my parents, instead of a doctor, my mother suggested that according to her research (that is, Google searches where every mother can earn her doctorate in medicine) it might have been anxiety. They left me with those words that evening after their treat of takeout Chipotle. I locked the door behind them of my one-bedroom apartment that was once so comfortable, and the walls seemed to be closing in on me. An incomprehensible sense of danger was before me and behind me, and inside me, and I couldn't gasp for enough air. My body was cold and hot, and I needed to scream, to yell for help but it was dark, and the world outside was no more assuring than it was where I stood, but I had to do something. I was alone, abandoned, unloved, and so desperate for anything but that. It occurred to me, sometime between my urgent fear of death and cold sweats, that I was having a panic attack. I couldn't put a face to any fear or threat I had encountered but the once so distant idea of *anxiety*. Eventually, somehow, air filtered back into my lungs and my reality changed into something more manageable. But the fear of going through that again loomed and for the ensuing few days the threat was ever-present and frequently rose by a racing heartbeat only to be subdued through a personal coaching session by the very same brain that was causing this trauma.

Naturally, this anxiety was consuming, but its source was unclear. I had to take an honest look at my environment, my perspective, the feelings I had seemed to glaze over with optimism as my body secretly suffered. The dawning of 2015 brought many changes to my environment, relationships, and understanding of the world. I moved into a new apartment where I officially emptied my childhood room and took the nameplate down, expecting never to claim it as my own again. I then lived by myself which, while it provided the solitude and freedoms I longed for, it also lacked the security of company when it mattered most—being ill or dying. This fear stemmed from the sudden death of a close friend's brother who died alone in his bathtub from heart failure at the young age of twenty-six the second month of that year. I began to see fatality more clearly as it moved within reach of my circumstances. I then understood in a more mortal way that anything can happen, including the change in relationships that leave us doubting what we once believed. I had a growing sense, after my voluntary separation from my childhood home, that my parents were no longer interested in the things I was doing or liked the person I was becoming, heightening my stress around them and deepening my longing for them. Meanwhile, I no longer found the same value in my closest relationships from college and questioned whether they would last, losing the security I once so adored about who we were together, and where we were going. The sands shifted beneath me and I wasn't handling it as well as I made myself believe. I was ashamed by that—that I wasn't undefeatable. I was also ashamed that my faith had not kept me from this suffering and that He wasn't the first one I turned to when I began this trial. But I came around and understood that this was one of my crosses to bear and I would carry that cross as I must.

That cross has been challenging. Though I have learned to settle many of the concerns that precipitated the symptoms and manage many of those symptoms that remain, I still struggle to lift my eyes from this world and recognize who is in control. There is a dichotomy between knowing and feeling this truth which often goes unreconciled in our hearts. As a laughable hypochondriac, I often consider a reaction to an unpredicted turn in health and, every time, suppose I would react with grace and biblical faith. But reality has made me a fool in comparison as I concern myself with matters outside my control.

My mom sat pretzel style across from me on her bed. She leaned forward and touched my nose where I told her I found a concerning bump.

"Oh my gosh!" she exclaimed cracking a smile.

"No, Mom, you're in the wrong the spot!" I grabbed her finger that tried to escape my home test and guided it onto the cyst that I was sure needed to be removed and would leave a horrible scar on the tip of my nose. She broke into laughter,

"Claire, there's nothing there!" I assured her she was wrong and she smiled with disbelief. "Claire, you need to stop worrying."

"What am I supposed to think when I faint? Something's not right. I can't just shake these new occurrences off."

"Honey, more than anyone I know, you've always had such a strong faith. Why do you worry?"

"I know everything's going to be okay, but there's this instinctual part of me that's freaking out when my body isn't working as it should. This is not normal for me. I grew up with a perfectly healthy body. I expected nothing but that. Now, my body is failing me in ways I never expected. Of course, I knew that could happen, but I didn't understand what it feels like to be betrayed until it happens. This is new to me. And it's scary."

I was entering dangerous territory with my brain, the one thing that controlled my fears and made me who I am and what I'm capable of and how I identify myself. I had seen how an illness in the brain could change a person and the way they interact with the world, limiting hearing or everyday functionality, and I was afraid of that, losing control over the thing that I believed made me completely who I was to the world.

I think the root of the problem was not that I worried incessantly but that I was still adjusting to the realization that my body was not perfect. As a child, my body was nothing but healthy. Day-to-day life was not stained by bodily questions or concerns. But following the young deaths around me and the new concerns about my own health, I was experiencing a different reality that was uncomfortable and simply uncharted. This, too, I had to hand to the Lord.

———

The conscious draw of breath is a reminder of your unity with God, and his desire for you, his love for you, and his will for you to draw another one.

Pavement

Encapsulated in the make-shift pavement lives we confine ourselves to, we mold to this illusory reality which tricks us into a relentless search for peace in our lives. The good roads only lead us so far and then we feel out of place as if we do not belong beyond them. We've created the false philosophy that life cannot exist far beyond their ceasing. So, we force ourselves deeper into the pavement.

Feel It

She sat in her wheelchair facing the TV, and I adjusted my chair towards her to encourage conversation. I began inquiring about day-to-day business at St. Therese's, her upscale nursing home. Grandma mentioned she would like to call more people, but it's hard for her to reach the phone, dial, and hear. She continued on about the challenge of being disconnected from old friends and distant family. She began to cry. I sat beside her watching the emotion flow from her eyes. My father tried to change the subject to a matter more heartwarming than heart-hurting. Understandably, he thought it was best for her to focus on the positive things about her days. I was agreeable but felt like he was trying to dry her eyes with sandpaper, scraping off the pieces of her existence that were so real and embedded into the folds of her wrinkles. I felt otherwise, that she needed to sit in it, to feel that emotion that was so worthy of her circumstance. For it is okay to cry. It is good to acknowledge the despair that enters our earthly life. When we accept it, we can use it to unite us more closely with the suffering Christ.

A VECTOR REUNION

I figured he might be there. I hoped he would, as not to make any conversation with him but for him to see me, happy, without him. And to my pleasure, he walked through that door. My heart didn't race, nor did my permeable stomach churn a hole inside of it. I had lost interest in speaking to him, so I didn't. But he tried, shortly after his grand entrance with supporters cheering his arrival. I glanced back to acknowledge his and Noel's presence and turned back around to continue the conversation that meant more than whatever value they had brought through that door. And soon, Cole was grazing his hand up the back of my head and leaning in for some sort of customary hug. I accepted, again with indifference.

He stared at me from across the room. I, in my thrift-store fur vest with matching fur heeled boots from Target, and he, well I can say he didn't even look half as good as me, and old, he looked old—worn from fatherhood and a lost dream. He laid back on the chaise resting on his palms spread far apart as if he was watching the sunset which was fitting considering my place in the room and my place in his heart. His eyes glazed over, and the sun beamed with pride in its wonder and power over its subject. And I, the sun, was setting on my hopes for us. The fire which lit our lives so brightly was settling into its new place, into the earth from which all things rise. I must anticipate its rising again but perhaps of another sort. For new love is on the horizon and will bear high in the sky a new day without the pain or thought of yesterday. I have greater days to behold and rise for. And as I nestle into my setting, I fear not the darkness for soon there will be light, and all things will be clear as the day dawns. But the one who held on to the promise of the sun was a mere boy who knew nothing of her timing or contents in her core. And so, he admired the sun's setting with a sweet song in his heart and prayer on his lips and watched her disappear.

Taylor, who sat on the arm of the couch four feet from Cole's same spot, motioned for me to come over. I sat down next to him, threw my arm around his shoulders and squeezed his right breast playfully. Cole said,

"Hi," again and we exchanged the usual interlude of greetings and responses as his eyes glazed over and his smile froze in place. I had nothing else to say to him nor wanted to continue the conversation, so we sat for perhaps a moment too long looking into each others' eyes. I prayed his girlfriend and best friend couldn't see through the facade we had rehearsed for so long.

The rest of the evening, I forgot he was there. Perhaps months earlier I would've tried to find reasons to talk to him and tried to engage in his life; alas, the sun had set. Perhaps it only took her time.

Chapter Five

Consideration

IOWA

I needed to throw-up or go to the bathroom. Jumping out of my seat, I panned the room for refuge. No, I needed to calm down. I just as quickly sat back down in an attempt to dismiss the feelings I had let swell within me. My mom and dad sat across from me, quietly eating the McDonald's breakfast meals I had paid for in gratitude for what they were about to do. An "Oh, shit!" moment crept into my muscles which were now tensing up without my permission. The aftershocks were wreaking havoc on the atmosphere. My car, which I wasn't sure would make it all the way to Iowa, waited outside for me, holding all the truly insignificant things that would get me through the next ten weeks. I couldn't breathe. It was all happening because I let it. I was packing up my life in Minneapolis and running to Iowa to work on a campaign with people I'd never met before, doing work I'd rather not be doing. I don't know why I do this to myself.

The opportunity came like a thief in the night. Just a few weeks prior, I came across a Facebook post by a "friend" whom I had never officially met. He befriended me after a brief email correspondence during Dave Baker's first campaign. I remember moments before, looking him up on Facebook, intrigued by his masculine name, and I delighted in his good looks. Overjoyed, I accepted the request I was too shy to make myself and anticipated our official meeting that was bound to happen considering the extensive list of mutual friends.

And I was right. After a few parties during which I was not brave enough to make the first introduction while slipping past him to get to the keg, I asked him to dance with me. Although I only know this through his portrayal of the incident, I guess he said no. He had just walked into the bar, and I was already lit. Thankfully, I was never the wiser about it, well, at least until I had already snagged him.

Months later, I saw his post on Facebook with a link to an article about him in the Minneapolis Star Tribune detailing his next adventure from the Minnesota Republican Party to a Rand Paul Political Action Committee (PAC) organizer. With Rand Paul as my pick for the 2016 presidential election, I was intrigued and curious as to what life in a PAC looked like and what life with the state party was like. In my own discontentment as a legislative assistant, I felt a particular calling to reach out to him and find out.

I changed my mind a few times, typing the LinkedIn message, then walking away from my desk with my hands on my head, fighting the urge to send it. I drafted and redrafted the message. A few hours later, I could no longer resist the Spirit—I could feel the resolution before my brain caught up, and I sent it. He quickly agreed to my request, and we set a meeting time for a few days later.

I was nervous to meet him but grateful it was for a special reason wherein we'd have particular content for our conversation and less of a chance for an awkward encounter (again, in my ignorance, I thought we hadn't had one of those yet). He was sitting in the back corner when I arrived—his back against the window with a cup to his lip. Prematurely hunched over in a perpetual shrug, he was reading his newly purchased slavery history book (something he never finished). We greeted one another cordially, I asked about the book, he admitted he had just started it, and we discussed his career path and my own career interests, and he excused himself after an hour. As we left Nina's, the corner coffee shop that was a result of a lucky Google search, I reflected on the openings in Iowa he had mentioned.

"Yeah, it probably isn't possible for me at this time," I said loosely, though I was certain the logistics were inconceivable.

"Well, keep it in mind."

"Sure..." and then I mumbled some awkward joke that he didn't understand, and he headed toward the next main street, and I walked deeper into the neighborhood. I got into my white, rust-stained Hyundai

Sonata (hoping he didn't see it) and cracked open the sunroof. Something suddenly felt different. It could have been the sun that I hadn't seen in six months, or perhaps it was the possibility that hung sweetly in the air.

The opportunity stuck to my shoes. As it was truly and solely voter contact, I was uninspired by the work. But the greater picture the work painted would hang appropriately on the walls at my funeral. I reviewed Ben's reasons for taking the opportunity and his own dance with the logistics and realized I might have written off the opportunity too soon. The "Oh, shit!" moments began to add up throughout the succeeding days as the impossible became possible. I decided to keep my apartment lease in Minnesota, have an open door at my current job, and sub-lease an affordable, temporary townhome in Iowa.

A few days later, on a quiet Friday afternoon, I sat around a small table at the Downtowner with my dad on my left and my mom on my right. They had promised to take me out to lunch after the legislative session to celebrate my year in politics, though it primarily served as a field trip for them and my grandpa who was so fond of old St. Paul. Time had demonstrated that it was moments like those, with my parents, that I found resolve. It was only three years earlier when I sat at my kitchen table, where most big decisions are made, realizing I could not make the move to Minot, ND to open a branch Vector office. Within a minute, my mom came in and told me that her and my dad didn't want me to go. They had always been supportive of the endeavor, but when the time drew near, something didn't feel right to them, nor did it to me, and we resolved that matter rather quickly. Years later, sitting at a different table, the players were still the same, and the stakes just as high. I was one step away from deciding the matter and was ready to resolve it. My stomach churned as I prepared to shake the words from my lips, confident I would be facing a fury of questions I had already asked myself, and I began.

"So you know how I mentioned I met a guy who is going to Iowa to work on a Rand Paul PAC? Well, he said there's room for me. And I'm thinking about doing it." Quicker than they had time to think, my mom and dad replied simultaneously.

"You should do it."

I was shocked by their confidence. My dad, the often more technically critical one, continued,

"It's a once in a lifetime opportunity, and your mom and I will support you in whatever way you need. If you need help paying rent here, anything." My mom agreed,

"It's a great opportunity." Still absorbing their reaction, I thanked them:

"Wow, I was nervous to tell you because your opinion is so important to me in making a decision like this. Thank you. I guess it's settled then." I proceeded to share the details of the arrangement, the timeline, and the mission, and we moved on to other things.

That following Tuesday, I received the acceptance letter from the PAC and approached my boss on Wednesday to reach an agreement on employment. I was terminated that Friday under the assumption that I would return later that year to my old position.

Two days later, I would find myself in an urban McDonald's about to lose my breakfast. The sickening energy may have come from the first bite of the McGriddle, but no breakfast sandwich would betray me like that—it must've been anticipation.

Ten minutes prior, when it was still too early to bear the shock of checking the clock, I walked to the dumpster through the grassy courtyard behind my apartment with the garbage bag that otherwise would have rotted over the succeeding months in my apartment, making the last exit from my apartment until only God knew when. I had put skin in the game, put it all on the line, took a leap and wondered, *what am I doing?* I didn't have an answer, so I carried the question with me.

Those "Oh, shit!" aftershocks were evident in Mom and Dad who sat across from me, still and speechless, in the middle of a Minneapolis McDonald's. I sat back down without a word and tried to stomach my sandwich as if Fear did not have a knife to my back and Anxiety was not waiting for me in the car.

This was my choice. I called Opportunity and welcomed her when she arrived; she brought Adventure, Excitement, Potential, and Value. She was a friend and a great blessing, but an equal burden.

Within five days, I quit my job, accepted a new one, picked up the pieces of my life I could grab with two arms, and moved to another state that was home to no one familiar and nothing known. Through it all, I bore the seal of the living on my chest and pronounced the name of Purpose. But assuredly, Fear and Anxiety hitched a ride on my sleeve and Faith on the sole of my shoes.

I was following a foreseeable passion and a gentle curiosity, trusting that it was a path meant for me at this time. It seems for most of my peers that is just what we do. We follow dreams and run towards finish lines. We yearn for an opportunity and grab it when it's within reach, and perhaps reach too far when it's not. We hope to do great things which often can lead us to feel lost and consistently unsettled. What else are we to do when the tiresome, survival-work has been done for us except pursue greater and nobler ventures?

So, I was out for a noble adventure, one that, for good or ill, had a man attached to it—Benjamin. We had met a few times within those past two weeks under the guise of discussing Iowa matters. Our relations slowly seemed to transition away from the intentions of networking and towards something equally adventurous.

DAWN

I was reluctant to start anything with him. Though I was drawn by his dark features and the storm behind his eyes, there was so much unknown about this man. After our first encounter at Nina's coffee house in St. Paul where he sat against the window sipping his coffee in between a line of questioning that I had already provided answers for and a few political discussions over beers, the unknown was slowly fading and so were my fantasies. Now, I had a personality to the face of both my informant and manager. Molding this relationship into one of the more intimate kind seemed dangerous—not to mention worthy of caution when letting anyone into such proximity.

I knew this forcefield needed to be breached eventually. Though I kept the field powerful enough to deter such a suitor as him, I kept sending him an invitation to move forward. For in our new town, I had no one else to send invitations to, and no excuses to lay out before him—no friends or family or work or social life to hide behind. So, his persistence bore us onward as I would sit across from him with narrowed eyes studying and observing and noting. I enjoyed the evenings we passed together as we explored our new city of Des Moines through our eyes and stomachs or spent those hours at either of our provisional homes, just being together. Slowly my coldness began to melt when he took my hand or nestled me into his fold, and I opened my heart to exploration. No moment distinctly taught me this was okay. Rather, through trial, I learned it was safe, and his constant nearness became a new normal. Through my perpetually single eyes, I began to see the delight in a relationship, and its goodness.

Soulmates

We came across a small group of teenagers who were looking for some sort of drug. I wasn't well acquainted with the drug scene in downtown Des Moines and offered my sympathies in their search. It was a summer night, full of hope and promise for us all. I encouraged them to stay in school, and we left them to their riverside endeavors. As we departed ways, one of the girls hollered back towards us,

"You guys are soulmates! You're adorable." I turned back, surprised by her insight, or rather, unsupported assumption. Ben kept walking, pulling me along towards the bridge. The cement walking-bridge supported our romancing. We looked out upon the new city and the new lives we found ourselves living. Ben wrapped his arms around me from behind and whispered in my ear,

"I'm so glad I found you." And as my heart delighted in these words, my mind feared them. Or perhaps my mind delighted, and my heart feared. I do struggle to understand the two.

Porn

I had to ask him the tough questions; questions I feared to know the answers to. I prayed that morning for the grace to have the conversation I needed to that day with Ben. I had the urge to ask a few different times and could not muster the courage. Finally, we were in the car heading away from the Capitol in Des Moines looking for a place to eat, when the radio personalities Ben had just turned on began discussing pornography. The first time they said the word "porn" I realized that was the chance I had prayed for, but waited in the silence called fear. They said the word again—poking, prodding me. I thought that would be my best chance. They said it again, and I spit it out:

"Do you watch porn?" The question hung in the air; he froze looking into his phone. He said,

"Let's go to El Bait Shop." I laughed with disappointment realizing what he was doing.

Both him and I compiled his response in our respective heads. Of course, when I had rehearsed asking the question, his answer was always "no." I initially presumed he did, as porn has been normalized among young men. But I hoped he would surprise me—he didn't. He watched porn and was surprised I didn't. Without getting into a tirade about my choice, I simply asked him to abstain from watching it while we were in a relationship. He agreed, and even tougher conversations were ahead of us.

———

Behold, we are created from Truth; thus, we contain the capacity to return to it.

DISAPPOINTMENT

Lord: I want to do what is good and right in your eyes. Heavenly Father, you know the contents and desires of my heart. You know what it needs and what it longs for and where it's going. Please guide it. Help me discern right from wrong. Lord, I feel compelled toward Ben for reasons I cannot explain. There was a longing and now a consuming. When we separate, it feels wrong and unnatural. I cannot remember what it was like before him. I lose my breath when I feel his distance, when I lack his attention, when the air between us thickens. But, somehow, I contemplate breaking up with him frequently and fear many things because of our differences in faith. Many have come to believe that if we believe in the same God, nothing more matters—it is the contents and applications of our faith that make the differences in doctrine null. But, these differences cannot be nullified so simply, they affect the way we think and the way we act, significantly guiding us. And I fear our faiths our guiding us toward different ends.

DISTRESS

I felt like we were in suspension. There were things that I needed to discuss with him, but I hid them behind my eyes, fearing their answers would force my hand and ours would unweave. But I couldn't stand that; I didn't want to let Ben go. Though I didn't know why I was holding him so tightly.

Our relationship wasn't progressing. We were spending every day together, and still I felt the distance of our souls, like they were kept behind glass walls. I put mine on display, desiring for it to be read and understood, but he didn't want to reach for it. He didn't want to hold it, tenderly. And my strongest identity, as a beloved of Christ, went unacknowledged. The greatest part of me was not embraced, but rather opposed, and I wondered if he could ever really love me for who I was and who I wanted to be.

I thought I had seen a light in him, a potential that could understand the great depth of my devotion and perhaps even want it for himself. So, I bore hope and trudged on with a prayer that my witness to the truth could be transformative. But I admit, with disappointment, that my hope wore thin at the raising of his voice and darkening of his eyes. I kept losing air—the contents of my soul were being suffocated behind the glass he kept me caged in.

CAV

He was bigger than I pictured Mr. Bolsen to be, taller and rounder. He struggled to move his heavy feet closer to the doorway and leaned into the glass door, opening it just enough to fully greet me with half-hearted interest.

"Hi there, are you Mr. Bolsen?" I asked, having rehearsed the same opening line, interchanging different family names, twenty-four thousand times over the course of the past four months.

Mr. Bolsen was perhaps the six-thousandth registered Republican I had greeted at their door (or in their yard, or through their upstairs window, or in their car, or in some awkward arrangement that began to not embarrass me any longer) during the primary race for the 2016 elections. Their responses were equally varied, though typically were some arrangement of "unsure" of whom they would support for the Republican nomination in the Iowa caucuses. And to my delight, mixed amongst the disinterested or rude or short-mannered or fearfully-hiding-behind-their-living-room-curtains, were the few that engaged in a meaningful conversation.

Some people just got it. They understood the system that drives governmental policy and were looking for a candidate that fought back against that. To most of these disillusioned voters, they thought a non-politician candidate would be a baby Jesus to Washington D.C. I stood there, one step below them, nodding my head. Frequently I'd add that Senator Rand Paul was the perfect mix of experience and outsider-thinking they were looking for in their next President. Yet, I remember people like Mike, who in the small town of Knoxville, saw a picture larger than his city limits. Mike had been involved, had stood on (perhaps not) as many doorsteps, and had glued himself to newspapers and TV screens to gain traction in fighting the system that still seemed to have an unacknowledged chokehold on its people. Both defeat and hope wrestled in the blink of his eye.

"Nothing ever changes," he lamented to this bright-eyed twenty-three-year-old who could only take his word for it,

"It doesn't matter who our candidate is. Nothing is going to change." Again, I nodded my head, understanding his sentiment, waiting for my chance to beam hope back into his line of vision. But I decided not to press him, figuring it would get us nowhere as he replayed his past fifty years of torment and frustration. So, I listened and left, putting this second-hand experience in my back pocket in case I ever wanted to take some time to chew on it. It wasn't infrequent that I encountered thinkers like Mike.

"None of them," Mr. Bolsen grumbled.

"That's unfortunate. There are so many candidates to choose from," I commented with a smile attempting to transition into my next question. But he grumbled on.

"Nothing ever changes."

"Well, sir, I think it can change," I added emphatically. His eyes narrowed, squeezing out the cynicism he had clearly built up over his years.

"It won't. All politicians are alike. You know what they are?"

"What?" I asked with a patient, lip-squeezing smile, not pleased to be humoring this grump.

"Liars! How can you support anyone?" He asked as if I was the enemy. He seemed to hate the idea of youthful hope. I could see why; hope can be irritating when it stands outside the faithless' prison and puts its thumb to its nose and waves its fingers.

"I'm not just supporting *anyone*. I'm supporting Rand Paul." He was getting frustrated with the unwavering sparkle in my eye and turned to belittlement before I could sell him on my candidate.

"What're you looking to get out of this anyway?" He prodded condescendingly, assuming it couldn't have been to get said political candidate elected. "Is it for a resume?"

"Sure, I'll put it on a resume," I shrugged in agreement. "But I wouldn't be doing this if I didn't believe in the transformative policies of Rand Paul."

"Honey, I have a few more years on you, and you'll see, it's always the same thing. You can't do anything about it."

"Maybe," I replied, stepping away from the door as to end the conversation, "but all I can do is try. Thanks for your time today, sir."

We peacefully exchanged adieus as I turned away and down his walk towards my next door. But the conversation followed me along the way, and every time I replayed it, my response grew in vigor. In my final version, I would have responded:

"I understand that very little has changed—many of the problems before us are still in view though time makes them look different and new. Maybe nothing will change. And sir, I'll probably be standing in your place one day saying the same thing to some young man or woman at my door. And I hope they say the same thing back to me—that things *can* change if we have the might to believe it and fight for it. Sir, you've given up on America. Somebody has to fight for her. And somebody someday will make a difference whether it's me or the next person at your doorstep. Someone just has to believe enough to make it happen. I'm just doing my part until that day comes."

That is what I was trying to convey in the brief conversation that felt both important and without effect, though only little can be grasped by those who think little. I don't believe Mr. Bolsen was entirely wrong, but he was part of the problem. When we don't believe in change, we will never fight for it.

I am almost certain that when I'm his age, I will have thrown out my worn-out sneakers and my last candidate's lit piece in frustration with the system that I insisted on fighting. Bloody and weak, I will recline, without interest in the spirited boy or girl on my doorstep. But in the meantime, in my own spiritedness and by my own supply of hope, I think it is reckless to see a problem and not seek its resolution—especially when the resolution is offering itself for our benefit.

PAIN

Ben: There are times I sit or stand next to you and feel lonely. Your cold selfishness penetrates my skin and freezes my heart; I want to run far from you, but I'm stuck on you. I try to count the number of times my heart turns away from you verses towards you in a day, and my distaste towards the things you do or the things you say outweigh the happiness I seldom feel in your presence or the joy of our conversation. I pace outside the hotel in the dark of the ending day exhaling my pains without any air to breathe. I've felt suffocated by the weight of our issues without firm ground to brace. But this helplessness, and silent pain, and frustration can be quickly forgotten in a wave of your smile and the comfort of your touch and makes me question what is actually important. So much of me is yearning to walk away and hold my head high with dignity and self-respect in protest of how I can feel unimportant and mistreated. Yet my hopefulness for you runs deep, and I stake it in Christ and His will for us. I don't expect you to be perfect or to say the perfect things or act in perfect ways, but I need to know that you will accept the reasonable feelings I have and not get upset with me in return. I desperately want to pour love into you, but I need to know there is no hole in your cup. Otherwise, this, all of this, will be to no avail.

M O M

We had just returned from Grandma and Grandpa's. Thirty minutes earlier, I was saying my farewells to a woman I hardly knew, and my sadness in doing so seemed guiltily obligatory. Yet, regardless of my lack of relationship with my grandma, she was my mom's mom. I should've harbored empathy for my mother who was losing hers, but I was not that wise. So, I sat motionless on the couch in the living room and watched my mom throw the cordless phone to the floor. She fell into pieces. Her scream echoed through my bones as I began to piece together what her dad had just told her on the other side of the phone. She began to bawl and sunk into the firm reclining chair. I sat and watched her dark loss.

I watched her a lot. I came to see many other emotions. And I, I came to believe I lacked the capacity for them.

I had been reviewing—swiftly, vaguely, and without particular conclusion—moments between Ben and me. I was recounting all the different emotions I had conjured up: jealousy, anger, frustration, love, concern, loneliness, entrapment, happiness, unhappiness, sadness, fear, hope, and other feelings for which I fail to find words. Reviewing such an extensive list made me question friends' assessment of me as being *unemotional.* At that time, I agreed with concern that I lacked the heart of a decent human being. Because of Ben, I began to see that I may have been wrong. Seeing the ease into which I could slip into a strong reaction helped me understand my mom and her experience as a wife and mother better to the point that I am embarrassed by my naivety. For

I could then place myself in her seat as she beams a quiet, painful glare out the passenger seat's window over some matter that meanders through the tunnels of her heart without certainty or resolve. I could then feel the ocean that overwhelms her at the failure of kindness when someone acts without consideration of her. I could then wrestle with the same demons and sit at the same table. Certainly, I could never fully walk her path, for it only belonged to her, but I was finding one very similar to hers wherein my frustration boiled beneath my skin as I tried to cool it down through silence and distant stares. Any little comment could trigger the upset, and every little gesture could excite the heart.

I imagined, too, that was why I grew to feel a particular closeness with her during my relationship with Ben. My emotions began to run more freely to her, and my openness revealed a new part of me of which I was fond. We bonded, as close as honey to its comb, as I shared my moments of doubt and fear and joy. I craved her assistance, finally understanding I was much more of a reflection of her than I had ever seen. And she was most interested in seeing what has reflected back to her; something I was sure she longed for during the years I turned away from her.

I love her dearly. She is outspokenly loving, steadily affirming, and overly generous. She is every child's dream. Nothing was spared or withheld. Memories of her feel as comforting as a summer's breeze and as pleasurable as the sound of the pizza man's knock on the door. The sound of her voice over the phone overwhelms me with the sense of contentment from the days she'd call home to check on us during summer vacation. There is nothing but goodness in her parenting; nothing more I could have asked for. I hope that I continue finding bits of her in me.

———

To what do we owe the beauty of the moon but to the radiance of the sun?

QUESTIONS

My heartspeak crawled and clawed at my throat. If I didn't let it out then, I feared I might not ever. Thankfully, the darkness let me hide for a few moments longer as I stood beside this man I desperately wanted to love me forever. The heartspeak grew feistier, and the clock added another minute to the night. I continued to rub in the sunscreen I unintelligibly used as a lotion while I discretely asked God for the courage to begin. And then I couldn't have stopped if I wanted to.

"Hey, Ben," I crawled onto the bed and peered over his back that felt like a brick wall. "Ben, I need to say something."

"Yeah," he said evenly, still tooling with his phone.

"Ben, can you look at me?" I pleaded, pulling him towards me, "Or at least try to." The darkness, again, was my protectress of vulnerability. Failing to make eye-contact in the meager spill of the parking-lot light through the curtains, I eased onto my side while pulling him onto his back and propped myself up on my elbow.

"You've recently made comments about us not having sex—"

"Yeah, yeah, it's nothing. I won't do that again." He waved it off defensively, trying to roll back onto his side and avoid conflict.

"No, no it's not that," I affirmed as I pulled him back. "I just want you to know that..." I breathed hoping I could conquer the fear in my tone, "I want you to know that I understand that it must be hard for you and if us not having sex is becoming a deal breaker for you, I need you to be upfront with me."

I could see the movement of his eyes through his eyelids as they searched back and forth for a response.

"I mean, it bothers me. But I knew that was your deal going into it."

"I know and I just, I just need you to be upfront with me if you get to a point where I'm not worth it anymore. Please, just break up with me before doing anything with anyone else."

"Is that what you want?" He asked. I probably should've just broken up with him right then, but I wasn't that sensible.

"No. No. I just want you to know that I don't want to be hurt. And if you realize down the road that it's not worth it to you, I want you to tell me that. I can take it," I claimed, unsure if he or I believed that. "Just don't cheat on me."

Those final words—expressing fear openly—cut sharply.

"I saw Paul for lunch in St. Paul and hung out the rest of the day..." his defense trailed off in my mind or perhaps I stopped listening as I tried to back-track.

"I don't suspect anything," though that might not have been true, "that's not it. I just want you to know that if the temptation was to arise, please don't hurt me."

"I would tell you," he confirmed without the dramatic espousal of commitment and love that I was really hoping for amidst my rising insecurities.

I laid onto my back with a sigh. I think it was a sigh of relief from having communicated my concerns, but to him, it sounded like one of disappointment.

"What? Was that not what you wanted to hear?" He asked rather confused.

I didn't know how to respond. For anyone who asks that seems to have aimed for the suitable response, rather than the real commentary, which fails to strike confidence in his or her audience. Regardless, what would have soothed my soul was for Benjamin to have first confided in his love for me and that he would never cheat on me, that I was worth waiting for, and that I was the only girl he wanted to be with. But in his rather realistic appetite, he merely promised he would tell me if he no longer wanted to wait for me. Though my romantic hopes were shattered by a dose of realism, I sincerely appreciated his honesty in matters of the heart. For in a worse case, I would wait outside his door, with no answer, no notification of change, bleeding and dying. Yet, though I could still bleed, his forgivable bluntness which I could count on too frequently would send me off to the hospital in time to heal.

I proceeded to tell him that I appreciated his promise to be honest with me and thanked him again for waiting as tears fell silently from my tired eyes. What he said *was* fine. But the matter remained: we placed different value on something that is so sacred to a relationship.

"It's not like some clock that's going to run out," he added unconvincingly.

"But it feels that way." I sniffled not sufficiently enough to catch the snot running down my nose as I attempted to conceal how deep the emotion ran. But he noticed.

"Are you crying?"

"No," I said as I thought I should say though we both knew the truth. His sincere show of affection eased the distance that I had created between us.

"Why are you sad?"

"I'm not, these are happy tears," I lied again, for reasons I still cannot understand, through sniffles. Sadness did not seem like an appropriate name for these tears—for it was despair over our future between a man who only saw the pleasure of sex and a woman who saw it as a covenantal act. With my short-sightedness, I could only see the ruin between two lovers of this sort. That was us. And the tears fell as I dwelled on our fate. Only a prayer and a miracle could save us. But I laid next to this man whose hand was running through the strands of my hair and I could only love him with the hope that one day, our eyes would not only meet but would see as one, eye-to-eye.

I believe that what I believe is right and good. I wished I did not wish to change how he saw the world. But there I laid, pleading for the heart of Jesus to consume his. I felt this desire deeply. I trust that what I wanted for him was good, not merely for my own sake, but for his, which made me wonder what it was that I loved about him in his current state. Was it simply him—as a soul, as it was? Could it have been my soul clinging to the essence of his and all it could be? Or was it more simple and unheroic? For though I have loved myself, and others, and God in the depths of the seas and valleys of singleness, perhaps I had come to adore the companionship of another and cowered at the idea of man's rejection. That alone, though a tragic human tale, could be the precipitant of the tears I had shed.

I knew it would be the journey to the end or the journey to a new beginning. In either case, I prayed it was a resolution of either. For I questioned, and toiled, and paced with the relationship I had with Benjamin. I had seen the way the Lord guided me through the years and was equally certain that he led me to Ben, rather pushed my steps into his. Though the journey with him was challenging considering the unique nature of us working together, it being my first real relationship, and the potentially insurmountable differences, I still had great hope in the power of the Lord. The world will tell me I am foolish to hope in changing a person. But my hope wasn't in changing man; it was in the Lord's power to change a person if it was in accordance with his will. The question then was: is the conversion of Ben to the understanding of sex and other consequential beliefs of Catholicism, and the values they instill, in the Lord's will?

I could not answer such a lofty question. So, I laid it at Christ's feet, asking him to break Ben's hardened heart and to give him sight into the goodness and truth of the faith, trusting that God's will would prevail. And I waited. I waited for my heart to surrender its patience or to see Ben's heart ignite in the tinder of truth. There was something within me that could not give up on him yet. Perhaps it was immaturity-driven or prodded by the Holy Spirit. I was reminded of the power of faith in Matthew 21:21-22 wherein Jesus says, "I tell you the truth. If you have faith and do not doubt, you will be able to do what I did to this tree. And you will be able to do more. You will be able to say to this mountain, 'Go, mountain, fall into the sea.' And if you have faith, it will happen. If you believe, you will get anything you ask for in prayer." I believe in the Lord's power to open the eyes of our hearts. I prayed, for the sake of our future, that this grace might be given to Ben.

THE WIND

The leaves skip down the street and dance upon the trees. I turn to watch, and its same force tousles my hair. I close my eyes as it floods over, flows around, and flies through me. My heart whispers, "I love you," as my God makes himself known—for his force is often gentle, sometimes powerful, essentially unseen, but seen by those who look. It is both quiet and loud. It is both warm and cool. It can be recognized through the observation of the moveable. It can be welcomed and it can not. But it is there nonetheless, boundless and concrete, present around me, making itself known, wanting to be known, wanting to be loved.

MORE QUESTIONS

I thought it was the hours of rehearsing the question in my car that threw a towel over our flaming chemistry. I knew I had to ask him that looming and determining question regarding our imaginary children: *"Ben, would you let me raise Julia and Paolo in the Catholic faith?"* I would ask as we laid side-by-side, me twirling the few inches of his hair between my fingers.

I was ready to face the question, the answer, and the consequences. I was craving resolve. I prepared myself for his answer, assuming "no" was the likelier response, and mixed in a few yeses to ease my troubled heart.

So, I entered his Iowa hotel room, after two days apart, with an eagerness and a false hopefulness, to alleviate any concern of our fate that was festering in my consciousness. Yet, something was still different. His affection had dissipated; from what test of elements I knew not. A new, more pertinent, question arose: what was going on with him?

As the evening of sharing stories from our days and making jokes about the ghost hunters on TV wore on, the evidence piled up. Something was off. He asked about my excitement for my trip to Cambodia and about my plans for next summer, questions that felt out of place—too formal for the level of our relationship. It turned out, he had his own concerns about us. He drew out his own fears by first handing me the remote then by handing me my glass of wine to finish, which I declined, intent on hearing his thoughts.

"I think with you going to Cambodia and me going to Florida in December and me not knowing what my job will entail, we should pump the breaks until we get back to Minnesota."

"Do you feel like we've been moving too fast?"

"Well, when you sent me your ring size on SnapChat it really hit me. I have no idea where I'll be after this. I could be anywhere."

"Ben, I know marriage is a long way off," I replied, embarrassed he felt that my casual gesture with a promotional coaster at a bar was aggressive. But that wasn't fair considering he had proposed to me three times before and had told me to move to Plymouth with him and settle down. I was just playing his game.

"I know you have a career to pursue," I added, repeating his own concerns.

"I've just been through this before. I told you, I was seeing a girl in Minnesota and moved to Virginia to work on another race. I was coming back, but she got married. It really made me depressed. Not clinically, but I was devastated." He waited for my response, then continued, "I guess that has made me a bit skittish."

"Look who's the skittish one now," I joked, hoping to lighten the mood. Another time of silence passed with both of us staring at the ceiling.

"You must think I'm really harsh for requesting this."

"No, I think I understand. I just wish I could protect my heart too." I didn't know how I could with him fencing off his, and me bearing mine openly awaiting his return. Then again, did mine need protecting? I was ready to let it feel something really true for the first time. Though I hadn't seriously prepared for the variety of directions his career could lead him, I didn't see what the harm would be of another month together. Perhaps he was just reconsidering us in the first place which led him to cut ties there and then. Perhaps he genuinely was conflicted by the uncertainty of a new job and was preparing for the worst. I could not quite read his heart yet; I could only listen to its verbalization. But even in those moments, I could get to know his heart and love it more. It was in those moments, listening to his heartspeak, that I grew closer to it and in it.

I debated on whether to throw in my question of the hour—would you let me raise our kids in the Catholic Church? But after his request to take the dangerous, Friends-episode-level of a break in our relationship, I wouldn't dare mention kids. I resolved to leave it for our negotiations when we were "back in Minnesota."

I can respect anyone's inclination to protect his or her heart for it can only bear so much at a time before it is rendered damaged. Yet, having mine with only the type of small scar that is forgotten with age, I still welcomed the feels, for they make me alive and tell me that I experienced something meaningful in this easily hollow existence.

I fretted over our conversation the next day. I heard nothing from him for forty-eight hours, even after his important career-changing meeting that would have addressed his concerns. My heart was slowly breaking into pieces as I tried to piece together what was happening between us. As the fragments came together, I began to see an image different from what he sketched it out to be. It looked more like rejection and dishonesty. The reality tore into me.

When we reunited in Mason City two days later, my heart was still heavy with confusion over us. We sat on opposite sides of the room making phone calls to voters. In between the calls, we would chat, though I was more reluctant to do so than he was. He asked if I wanted to watch the Borgias or the documentary he suggested that night.

"What do you want to do?" He asked.

I sighed in distress, confused as to why he suggested doing that or anything together.

"I want to know what's going on with us," I blurted out with angst. A woman picked up the phone, and I went into my script, abandoning the conversation with Ben. Throughout the next few calls, I rehearsed what exactly it was that I wanted him to know. And when I finally put it together—knowing well it probably wasn't everything I should say to him—I took out my earbuds.

"Ben, I just want you to know that I hate what we're doing. I feel constantly stuck between being hurt and being mad at you. It's confusing, and it hurts, and I hate it."

He sat there waiting for his next call to pick up.

"Want to talk about this tonight?" He asked. Relieved I got that off my chest, I put my earbuds back in and proceeded with my next call.

As night came around, we both knew that we should talk about it, but neither of us really knew what to say. Every hour that passed I thought about that conversation we were supposed to be having and anxiously let the next hour come. I knew not what to bring up first or what objective to aim for. Changing his mind wasn't necessarily on the table nor was changing how I felt about it.

The next day came, and not a word of importance had been exchanged between us. The small talk eventually turned into our normal banter, and I received some grace to endure the next few days. Too much energy was allotted to my heart, and my stomach began to ache. Upon our entry into Mason City, I canvassed with a sharp pain in my stomach. Dismissing it as stomach gas, I tried to drink lots of water. Days passed without relief, and it began to concern this relatively healthy twenty-three-year-old. A quick decision to return to the Twin Cities for medical care led me out of Iowa for the last time with Concerned American Voters (CAV). After learning I potentially had an ulcer or gastritis, I cut my ties with CAV to escape the rejection I faced with the sunrise and the sunset and to heal before my trip abroad for my brother Philip's wedding. Little did I know, that would be my last time with CAV, but the time away gave me a new perspective on Ben—one that was desperately needed.

YEAR OF MERCY

It had already been a challenging Year of Mercy. Sweating in my traditional Cambodian wedding attire, I paced back and forth outside of the reception hall listening to my parents who were eight-thousand miles away worrying about Alex.

"We don't know how much Alex has told you, but he's having a panic attack. He's been texting us about wanting to fly home as soon as possible. He needs to get out of there."

"Okay," I inserted impatiently, waiting for their intrusive plan.

"Would you be okay with coming home early?"

"Well, let's just wait to find out when we can even get a flight home and talk about it then." They paused considering my response.

"Talk to him and make sure he's alright. When he called us, he was fighting back tears," my mom said with worry in her voice. I rolled my eyes in frustration. I didn't know what they expected me to accomplish; they knew what Alex thought of me. Admittedly, I was concerned too. I knew the awful, death-anticipating feeling a panic attack strikes and was reminded of my call to act mercifully during the Church's Year of Mercy. I could reach out and hold his hand (clearly metaphorically) or distance myself as much as possible from my ailing brother. After accomplishing very little on the phone, since their demands were unwelcome and non-actionable, I dismissed my parents so I could get back to greeting the wedding guests.

Alex unhappily sat across from me in the makeshift entryway draped in colorful fabrics and carpeted in red. Between the waists of guests passing between us, he asked,

"Would you be okay going home tomorrow?" Naturally, after having gotten sick from the food a few days earlier, I was looking forward to going home, but not on the timeline Alex was proposing.

"Let's just wait and see when we can get a flight out," I responded, avoiding committing to a plan. Moments later, after thinking about how much I didn't want to leave without seeing Angkor Wat (the primary tourist attraction in Cambodia), I asked him if he'd be okay flying home alone. Likely out of pride, he answered that he would be; moments later he added,

"But Mom and Dad said we couldn't travel alone." As much as I respect my parents, I didn't care what they commanded this twenty-something to do and took Alex's response to mean he really didn't want to travel alone. So, I was faced with a predicament: do I make a decision to fly home early based on my own convenience—only if we still had a day to see Angkor Wat—or, out of mercy for Alex, do I agree to leave the earliest we could get a flight home? Waiting to make the decision was no act of mercy, it was for my convenience. For that, I was ashamed, knowing that my willingness to return my brother to safety was inhibited by my selfishness.

I sat debating the predicament, rising every-so-often to help pass out glass ornament wedding favors. The guests' faces would light up as they noticed our differing ethnicities and I would join my hands at my chin and bow my head slightly whispering a butchered Kamai greeting. They would laugh and repeat my greeting with better pronunciation and continue to their tables that were prepared for a multiple course, family-style meal. It was Philip and Sokunthea's wedding reception.

The Tiger beer ran freely that night around the tables. Men were seen carrying out cases of it, passing the cans around until everyone had one with which to cheers. The beer was warm and passable as any standard alcoholic beverage. Our new uncle-in-law put cans on ice for us foreigners who liked it cold but couldn't contaminate the drink with local water; *it was the thought that counted,* I reminded myself as I drank his unsuccessful attempt. I was just happy to have made it to this day. Alex and Philip were at a nearby roundtable laughing with a group of guys over what I'm not sure anyone knew. They were having fun. We took to the dance floor that featured a crystal table with an ornate fruit display that was ransacked by the end of the night. We danced around it to both eastern and western beats, forming circles around showstoppers and lip-syncing with our favorite tunes. By the end of the night, the chairs were stacked, and the marble floor was littered with dirty napkins and stray palm branches.

After that night, my wonderment of the Kamai people remained and so did my disappointment in failing to show mercy to my brother. And still, our Lord shows mercy unto me, and surely how little I deserve it.

———

Our souls are precious, and so is the time we spend on them.

RETURN TO ME

"Good luck to you and Kathleen on your alumni angle, take care," he wrote, sharpening his blade. The first few drafts of my response were unsuitable for a woman who would one day have to account for her words. Before I could sufficiently edit my own attack, he advanced another one:

"I know I'm supposed to marry you and do whatever you tell me to do, but I'm sure you'll find a suitable bro soon." My heart began to race, and my feet tried to keep up as I paced across my Minneapolis apartment. I crossed back to the couch in disbelief of his boldness and read it again. And again, I began drafting my response and editing it down, eliminating the expletives, leaving nothing left. I breathed, and breathed again. I didn't know what to say, so I called him—no answer.

I was running out of breath. I didn't deserve this and hated that he thought it was okay to speak that way to me, let alone think those things of me when I had been nothing but good to him. For days, I had contemplated a fast from talking to him during our break but was too meek to suggest it—after all, confrontation was what I was trying to avoid during this period of texting that dug us into miscommunication holes. But I wasn't quick enough to suggest it. So, I laid in bed, my hands on my head as if they could pull out the appropriate response to knock this boy off his high horse. Then I thought of something and questioned its repercussions, and perhaps resolved too quickly to respond to him:

"Grow up. Don't talk to me." And I began to formulate the letter I would send to him the next day:

~~Dear Benjamin,~~

Ben:

I laid next to your stream of incoming text messages. Between each, sending a prayer that you might start fighting for me. With each, raising my head to check as my heart fell to my stomach—nope, nothing, not yet. My heart wrestled with my spirit, one fighting to stand up for myself, the other fighting to wait it out. The other prevailed.

So, I laid in this field with your warfare, just taking it. I wouldn't fight back this time. I was too wounded and worn down from the war. I believed it was waged by insecurity; understandable, but unjustified. I didn't want this to be our history, but alas, I don't think it could have been written any other way—for my heart is too gentle and too willing. It cannot bear uncertain goodbyes, and cannot qualify many with certainty. It cannot give up without tried reason. It does not let go easily. But it is earnest and accepting of its fate. I have to remind myself of your faults and failures regularly, without excuse. And perhaps, I am grateful for those very faults and failures that provided a firmer foundation to see you off from. Otherwise, I would have fought for us until my fingertips bled on the beads of my faith and used its rope to keep your ship at bay.

You were ruinous, assuming what could not be conceived in my own thoughts. You were a creator, fabricating a person projected upon me whom I knew not. You were unrelenting. And to consider that you began this facade hurts the most. You broke up with me, wanting to put the breaks on, then started picturing me on the prowl with my one-night hookup list and turning me into some second-rate version without probable cause, diluting any hope of us trying again. It could have been different.

I have not ceased turning to our Lord for guidance, and hope that this is his hand guiding you out to sea. But there's still a part of me, yes—there is, that is reaching out towards you as far as I can stretch. Regret weighs on me, and I cannot feel the Spirit either lifting it or pressing it upon me. So, I stand here with my feet cemented to the shoreline, and my arms stretched out toward you. Yet, you, you sail on with the wind, your hands at the helm, doing nothing to return to me when all along, that was all I sent you off for—to return to me.

A GOODBYE

And suddenly I had nothing left to say. Nor did I care to stretch my tired arm into the crevasses that were our futures and pull something out. My heart yearned not, and my body followed course, and I wondered what might be running through his mind since my lack of words left the pages silent. Could he feel it too? Did my hesitancy bleed through the keyboard of my phone?

I did not care, either way, for finally I felt resolute. That is what my heart longest yearned for. My feelings faded, and I could no longer imagine the colors that once painted the house my heart dwelled in. I do remember often questioning its foundation and fretting over its structure, praying for its durability as I carefully colored its walls in shades of dreams and promise.

Eventually, I rested, turning towards the windows with withered panes and took in its picture. I realized that I, rather, wanted to dance with the leaves and revel in the sun on the other side of that glass. I suppose I had always known that. The heart always knows what it wants. But it is our minds that become entrapped by circumstance and possibility. I don't know how the heart finally overshadows, but am grateful when it does. So somewhere between painting and peering, my heart accepted this was no suitable home for it. It could decorate and plan all it desired, but it'd still be in the same house, with the same foundation. I no longer saw the potential and the bright colors that drowned out the darkness. They faded. As the sun set so did the light within the house we built. So, I stepped out onto the street and began to walk onward, looking for a new home to dwell.

Each passing day was a victory over death, and only that. In the cage that I kept myself captive, as his selfishness poured through the iron bars, his bitterness saturating everything I owned, and his presence radiating an equal dose of discomfort and doubt, I tallied each setting sun. And in its absence, I laid alone screaming, drowning out the voices in my head that spoke in every language but my own, waiting for the sun to return and sit upon the horizon, calling out to me: "Just hold on another day."

But my strength comes not from understanding; it rides on the stallion of hope—that I might come to understand, and that things are good, or becoming so. For if, and when, understanding bears down on me, it frees me, and there is no need for strength, only courage to experience the freedom I knew not of for so long.

As my stomach churned for freedom, so I sought it in the most resolute way. Though the roads were dark and many, I employed my spirit to guide me towards the scent of peace. Even the right road may only present the faintest telling as it is clouded with the fog of sadness and doubt, but it is there nonetheless and grows stronger with every step towards freedom.

I thought I found it. Then I took it. The night I returned from my trip to Cambodia, I asked if he was free the next evening. As much as I didn't want to talk to him, I was confident speaking to him in person about the matter, even if it took forty-five seconds, would be better than the text war that would likely ensue. But he didn't have time for me. He had errands to run after we had been apart for a month and a half. He suggested seeing one another Friday, but I was planning on meeting my future husband that night; so, I was busy.

"Can't Friday. I wanted to talk face-to-face because I don't think we're going to work out. So, if you want to talk about it, you can swing by tonight," I texted him after my mom edited it as I read it aloud to her in the kitchen.

"What more is there to talk about?" He asked. He had no interest in stopping me from tearing down our house. He might as well have offered to help. I guess he did when he name-called, accused, and blocked me from contact with him shortly after that. If I wasn't sure already, he certainly gave me the thumbs up when he stuck his middle finger up.

Yet, I still waited for him to text me with the hope of having me back; I even would excite when I heard the mailman. It would change nothing, but I'd have the pleasure of knowing I meant something to him and that he'd rather have me back than not, though I'm sure he felt the same. But with each passing day, as the silence grew longer, I grew with certainty that there is something better out there waiting for me.

THE PROMISE

She told me when they got married they promised one another they would never get a divorce. I held onto that promise like a blankie as I sat on the ninth stair, just behind the protruding staircase wall, within earshot of my parents blowing smoke in the kitchen.

Their words, and our tears, flooded our house and nearly drowned me. But they had stowed away a life preserver, assuring me that no matter how high the waters got, they would subside and we would survive.

And we did.

They made a promise that upon dissection seems rather redundant. Mom and Dad took marriage vows, the very ones that say, "...until death do us part," then promised they would never let anything but death part them, particularly by means of a divorce. As a child, I clung to that pacifier. As an adult, I admire their foresight of the times in which they would battle and their resistance to anything that accepted hardened hearts as final.

Our culture has made marriage into a transient commitment subject to everything but the vows that established that commitment. My parents saw that and declared that divorce would not be an option for them when the waters rose to their necks. Instead, they clung to commitment and believed the sun was behind those clouds and could dry up their tears. They chose to wait out the rainstorm.

I thank them for their commitment and cannot speak for anyone but myself on this matter though I will always hold true the power of endurance and most assuredly, God, in a marriage. With great hope, I view marriage as the strongest presence of Christ in this world wherein we commit fully to the person we wed, as Jesus commits fully to us. It is quite the challenge and no small battle, but it is the best thing we can do—the greatest human achievement to bond yourself freely to the life of another, offering everything you have and even more when darkness falls, rising from the ashes of this world arm-and-arm with one who is flawed, as much as you are. The journey of marriage may be the greatest human achievement.

The Letter

For four weeks, I had been waiting for it. I checked the mailbox in anticipation each day after work, closing it seconds later, shaking off my disappointment that it remained empty without the words that I both longed and dreaded to hear. *It wouldn't have arrived yet,* I would try telling myself as I inserted the short key into the third mailbox. Managing my expectations was easy, understanding what they really were was a much more arduous task that I hadn't let myself undertake.

Eventually, it had to come. With my lunchtime TjMaxx purchases in tow, I snatched the thick, white envelope from my mailbox and carried it up the stairs only to throw it on the floor of my living room, awaiting my attention. I put my new candles in place, the new teapot I snagged on clearance on the stove top, and my cookbook in its new easel as the white wine chilled in the freezer. Patiently, I put my home in order to the tune of my eight-tracks "sad + love" playlists and poured a large glass of wine as my mind raced in circles from anticipation to eagerness to dread back to anticipation. Without an understanding of my hopes for this letter—what it was to accomplish or what it might say—I settled into the center cushion of the couch and opened the envelope.

My eyes widened as the number of pages totaled five, covered in cursive penmanship. Passing over the different pages, the top line on the fourth page caught my eye:

I was foolish to do anything but marry you.

I lost my breath and hid the words with its preceding companions. I started over, from the beginning.

Digesting his lyrical telling of our story did little more than it might do to a stranger reading his work. It was sweet and romantic, yet uninspiring. Ben's words, full of promise and infatuation, were unreciprocated. So, it read as a pleasing addendum to a sappy RomCom, and my loneliness tempted me to jump into the story too, believing it was real and mutual and foolproof.

Luckily, my religious discipline has strengthened me against the dark arts of temptation and has taught me reasonable deduction, moral codes, and the map of the Spirit (though, arguably, the latter will never be fully understood). With these tools, I let go of the letter and lifted my hands with a prayer that they might return to my bosom filled with peace and a plan.

I am considerably patient with the matters of the heart, though I felt a timer was embedded into my back, eager to have a response for the one who bore his heart at the door of mine. I could not tell what I wanted or what I should do. His letter changed nothing—I already knew he genuinely liked me. He didn't give me any court-worthy arguments to jump in again. Yet, I awaited those pages daily, without growing tired, with a promise, or simply an understanding, that they *should* change things between Ben and me.

The way he treated me drove me to the edge of our relationship; I jumped off because of my inability to desire him at a moment when I felt most alive—dancing around the pile of fruit that mocked a traditional wedding cake in a sea of Cambodians wearing a beautiful gown and moving to the beat of the living. It's not true that I couldn't picture him next to me, I believe my imagination is able enough for such craftiness; it was that I didn't *want* him there. Instead of wanting to experience this height of happiness with him, I believed it would have been worse with him next to me. As depressing as the feeling was to admit, I was freed. My feelings for him no longer interrupted my judgment, rather they, once transformed, closed our case. The future arguments to be made or rebutted, the list of concerns that laid yet to be checked off, the differences that never clearly established themselves as good or bad, were no longer of use in the courtroom. ~~We were~~ I was done.

Meanwhile, I filed his poor behavior towards me under "long-distance stress" and the way it seeps into people's brains and makes it swell, deadening their decision-making and provoking their insecurities. The behavior is never excusable, but in mercy, I could see the hurt and pain he was masking. His words, then, were rather, and unfortunately, the shields (or perhaps the weaponry) he used in his battle for my love.

So, I took a few steps back from the edge to assess the view.

Still, I saw the many days I felt lonely by his side, the nights I felt insecure in our relationship, the moments he left me standing without a knight, the breakup conversations I was too reluctant to have, the distaste I had in parts of our everyday life, the doubts I conjured in his ability to love me, and the many times I felt uncomfortable and out of place. Was that part of every landscape? Were these the growing pains of relationships? I toiled, thinking I should feel certain. I debated a new agreement.

If I stepped away from the edge, how likely was I, given our new working and living arrangements in the Twin Cities, to return to that edge and recall my reason for jumping? Or worse, what if I never stepped away to learn whether things could be different in our new season of living?

I relent that in the "never again" to the "tried again," given two similar options in any other circumstance, I would advise the latter—to try again. But I risked entangling my heart and mind in us, making it difficult to walk away if I needed to.

I was bewildered and numb. My heart was forgiving, my mind, less so. A response was certainly warranted but what it would entail was not as clear as I shuffled the pages around trying to scan the words and shake out their consequences. Nothing fell out, and so I bought more time.

"Thank you for your letter. I'll call you later," I texted the 407 number that never again found a contact in my phone. "Later" turned into "days later" as I wrestled restlessly with Prudence. In the end, I asked for more time relenting that I still carried concerns and didn't want to play with his heart. He mocked my judiciousness:

"It's not like you're going into the desert for forty days," though that is exactly what my heart intended to do.

As my relationship began through the promptings of the spirit, so I thought it might end as my heart ventured into the desert with the Lord waiting for its call. The call came a week later as I stood in a pew amongst strangers and kin and my mind drifted to him, and a need to see him, face-to-face on different terms than a book exchange too quickly after "we're not going to work out." The feeling was persistent and nagging, and my heart resisted not. I thanked the Lord for this step towards resolution, trusting in His will and great design.

We met a few days later. I drove through a snow storm to meet in his city and waited ten minutes too long for his arrival from his place not three blocks from the bar. As I waited, I recounted the many times we had done this before—me waiting for the arrival of a man that really wasn't worth waiting for. And the night pursued in the frame of this setting. It was great catching up with my friend, but my friend might never become more than that again.

"When can I see you again?" he asked standing in the snowfall with his hands folded reservedly into his NorthFace, his face extra dopey. Unconvinced myself, I answered,

"Mmm, maybe next week?"

Yet, a week turned into two and I hardly noticed. My heart wandered back into the desert and swam in the mirage of peace. Interest in seeing him again dissolved in the mirage, and I wandered out ready to move on. Though, I will give him some credit in my resolution since his accusatory texts continued to make their way to my inbox and my desire to deal with the drama pushed them right into the outbox along with his phone number. So, a few days later when the courage set in, I sent him a DM (direct message) on Twitter saying,

"I'm out."

He said, "I thought you'd call."

I said, "I no longer have your number."

And that was the last I considered him.

WALLS OF THE INTERIOR

There's a great peace in entering the interior. It is inside that we can see the pieces that join to tell the hours of our day. When we see that each piece has a place in the mind of God, so small we would see them unfit for such a Wonder, yet still displayed on the walls to pronounce their purpose, it is then that we see the temple that we are and the glorious love of our Father.

A PLEA

On what ground can I stand and scream "Lead me!" as the pages of your Word flutter in the wind all around me? They are constantly about me within an arm's length whispering The Way. And I in the fury, drown out every voice by my own, screaming louder with greater resolve, "Lord, lead me!"

Through His silence, he answers—how he already has, is, and plans. I see I need no more than that and the pages fall, scattered around my feet. I sit and begin to reread. How that we both desire holiness for me is driven along one path, that of Jesus asking me to pray, love, confess, gather and carry my crosses. Everything else seemingly unrelated is either indeed related or insignificant, for his hand is always outstretched. I ask him to lead when that is what he already wants to do; he is asking me to follow. It is easier to be led than to follow—though seemingly the same, it is a matter of what action we focus on: the act of submitting to follow despite my own foreseeable pathways or the act of letting the one who knows the way lead me. Ah, the second is a much more peaceful way.

It is when my heart pleas that I silence it to listen to the voice of our Father and let him lead me as he already has, already is, and already plans to do.

TWENTY-THREE

Michael Jordan knew the number represented greatness. Though alone, it means nothing; on the back of a dreamer, it could mean anything. It could represent hard work and strategic thinking; it could symbolize courage and faith; it could brand hope and adventure into its bearer. And I, longing for all of those things, took on the number twenty-three with sincere humility, accepting that, in bearing this powerful number, anything could happen in the next year.

Anything can happen.

Rest in the power of that truth. It's a truth that can be waved away with the heaviest roll of eyes or stun our master perceptions of reality to a sobering dumbfoundedness. As I stood in the back of my senior party watching images of my class's dance with college flash across the screen and recounting my own, I felt it—the possibility that anything can happen.

But at the same time, absolutely nothing can happen. Time refuses to wait for the unintentional, and our days can mold into years that can only speak to the hours spent horizontal or those exhausted within four walls of complacency. Yet, time could also speak to wisdom and experience, accomplishment and growth. Time can be a slanderous enemy or your best advocate.

That is what I chose to celebrate twenty-three years after the day of my birth, and the succeeding days that led to the next candle atop my cake—the promise of uncertainty. And perhaps not surprisingly, amidst the balloons and streamers and the Beyonce playlist on repeat, uncertainty was delivered multiple times between twenty-three and its much older and wiser successor, twenty-four: I quit a job unexpectedly and began a new one before the next Sunday came, I fell in love, I fell out of love, I lived out of innumerable Iowan hotel rooms, I traveled across the world, I suffered, I rejoiced, I witnessed others doing much of the same and not, and life unfolded in patterns I had never seen before.

It was but another addition to the quilt that puts me to rest at night and wakes with me at the dawn of a new day. And yet, despite every new, seemingly unrelated pattern added between the markers of my life, this quilt is becoming something magnificent.

This quilt—these pieces—has shown me both the heights and depths of humanity, both what is possible and what I wish was not, and as I sit in this reality, I have become more entrenched in its questions and its snares. I have spent nights on my couch after work battling between my desire to do something and my will that detests. Weekends have passed without any sketches in a planner.

I chose to celebrate the 365 days that passed, and all that happened within them. I chose to celebrate the 365 to come, and all that would happen among them. I chose to celebrate the very moment in which I straddle the old and the new. For we are the compilation of our past, our present, and our future, a coalition that strengthens every single day to help us become our best, our finest, and our fullest. May we always believe the best is yet to come as we put on our number and bear it with purpose, intention, and the hope of possibility.

EVENTS

I came home from a bonfire—having roasted my skin enough to keep the Minnesotan mosquitos off my back, packed chair-to-chair amongst my old friends from church—and sat down on my couch with my laptop to scroll through the latest commentary, share-worthy news, and less-than-noteworthy updates by friends on Facebook. Within those past few days, seventy percent of any circulated information would undoubtedly contribute to one of the storylines my children will read about in their history books. I wondered what they might imagine these times looked like. I wondered what will become of us, the ones breathing in that heavy air.

Though my daily duties largely remained unaffected by even the most appalling incidences within my city limits, through these incidences, I had been conditioned into new expectations. As I would move between my bathroom and bedroom preparing for bed and hear sirens, I no longer simply considered the likely case of emergency services responding to a car crash, house fire, or burglary. I was conditioned to wonder what mass shooting might have been taking place—who initiated it, who it victimized, or perhaps what violent protest or riot might have broken out on the surrounding city streets. Perhaps it was then that my ignorance had been buffed away by the repeating narratives that I heard more clearly as an adult. Yet, more significant than my developed hearing is our developed world.

Our world is certainly a captivating wonder filled with beauty, grace, and love. It will always possess the potential for goodness and life. Today, that truth remains difficult to honor, veiled by fear, danger, and unrest. Yes, danger looms. Danger threatens the society our ancestors worked to establish. We cannot live in fear, for then they have one. We must live with hope. I have faith that even in the most dangerous of societies, our God is still God. Yes, in the face of danger, we shall hope in our Heavenly Father. Still, there is an inherent discomfort in the sirens that reverberate within my apartment walls and send chills down my back. There is an uneasiness about instability and having to live through it, even with the assurance of a savior.

So, I wonder what our kids will think about these days and if they'll have days like these and if they'll wonder about their future like we so often wonder about ours and like our mothers and fathers wondered about theirs and like history wondered about us.

OFFICE

One Tuesday morning was average by any first telling. I had made two fried eggs with hot sauce for breakfast and was trying to make my unwashed hair presentable when I received a rare phone call from a colleague. Curious, I answered.

"Hey, who's district do you live in?" Adam asked.

"Uhhh, I'm not sure," I responded turning to my computer to input my address on District Finder, a bookmarked website I used at work for every constituent caller. I amended my response:

"Sixty-Two A."

"Uh—okay, yeah that's Karen Clark's district. Can you file to run?"

"Um, no? I don't know? Can I think about it?"

"Yeah, but you need to file by 4:30 p.m. today. You don't have to do anything. We just want to have someone running against her."

"Okay. Let me think about it, and I'll get back to you."

So, I thought about it. I thought about running for public office. I had considered it before like any young politico has, but that vision included a husband, kids, and a home in a Republican-leaning suburb. Now, I'm a single woman living in an apartment in the most Democratic district in Minnesota considering my candidacy. Clearly, I was not going to win if I did put my name on the ballot, but my name was needed. I spoke with some colleagues over lunch about the effect a bid that year could have on my political future (if there was a future for me in politics) and what expectations the caucus would have for my race. Our chief-of-staff reflected my concerns and eased them, though I recognized he likely wanted my name on the ballot more than he wanted to share impartial information. Still, the risks were low—primarily requiring my time, and if my campaign laid low, I wouldn't have any trouble in potential future elections.

I prayed fervently throughout the next few hours while debating the costs and benefits. As time wore on, I began to piece together my decision—I understood they needed me and lacked strong reasons to decline the opportunity. I said,

"Lord, please stop me from doing this if this is against your will." And he didn't. At the end of the day, I took one hundred dollars out of the ATM, went to the first floor of the State Office Building to the Secretary of State's Office, and asked for the paperwork to file for office. My head was spinning. I was officially a candidate for State Representative.

The succeeding months were dull for this House Candidate. I received a few checks in the mail, and visits to my Facebook page. I established a website and had professional candidate photos taken by a friend from church. The Senate District Sixty-Two Chair, Bruce Lund, was a useful resource for collecting a list of local Republican potential donors. In six months, we raised about twenty-five hundred dollars, though one thousand of it came from a sweet, retired man named Mark who also included in the envelope a Miraculous Medal and an informational pamphlet about how your diet can cure cancer (both of which I greatly appreciated). We spent two hundred dollars on campaign t-shirts that served no purpose and another fifteen hundred dollars on a postcard that might have gotten me over my goal of ten percent (I received eleven percent of the total vote, a total of sixteen hundred votes). Surprisingly, or not, that percentage was the highest for a Republican candidate in the previous six years. I considered it a victory.

I don't know what any of it was for. I don't have room for candidacy on my resume nor would I find it a good selling point. I didn't take office or make any significant connections. I didn't further the conservative message in the district or provide the local party with better data or a better image. Perhaps some experiences are meant to pass with a shrug, or perhaps their purpose simply takes time to uncover.

THE INEVITABLE

Kelly had devised the perfect plan to attend the party of the year—the Republican National Convention (RNC). According to her sources, the RNC was a hub for single, Republican men (though they probably didn't think the same about the women). Her plan began at the local caucuses on March 1st where we would get elected to be delegates to the Senate Convention, where we could then be elected as delegates to the Congressional Convention, where we could finally become delegates to the RNC. The plan sounded fool-proof—that was, if I was committed to it.

By the time March 1st rolled around, the candidate I had worked so hard for the previous summer was out of the race and the remaining three contenders—Trump, Cruz, and Rubio—were uninspiring. I didn't know who to caucus for, and the chance of being elected a national delegate in perhaps the most contentious race in GOP modern history was highly improbable. Against her wishes, I neglected to attend and instead grabbed a beer with a friend.

A month later, Kelly again encouraged me to do something I wouldn't have otherwise done. Together we attended the Young Republicans Convention for the socializing opportunity—in my ignorance, I thought the convention was unrelated to the events surrounding the other conventions happening around the state. Partway through the makeshift meeting, Kelly and I huddled with our fellow Congressional District Five activists in the corner. There was a Democrat amongst us, the girlfriend of one of the board members of the Young Republicans. I never understood those who could couple-up with people of such different perspectives but admire those who venture into such looming challenges. Regardless, she was in our small group of ten or so. The chair of our congressional district was in our midst that day leading the election of the Young Republican delegates to the convention in a month. He opened the floor to nominations during which I nominated Kelly to be a delegate as she requested. Erin, the Democrat, asked if I had been nominated to which I admitted I hadn't. She continued with a brief rant that more women needed to be involved in politics which I was offended by considering I worked in government, staffed campaigns, and was present at the convention. Oh, how I loathe taking offense and repeat Abraham Lincoln's words in my shame: "We should be too big to take offense and too noble to give it." Plus, I was sure it was the Lord's prompting—she then nominated me to be an alternate delegate. Immediately, Kelly brewed another idea.

"Claire! We can still do it! We can still run to be national delegates!" Surprised her dream was still alive and warming to the idea myself, I excitedly agreed to pursue her old plan.

The Saturday of that Senate Convention rolled around on a warm spring morning—well, warm by Minnesotan standards. Kelly picked me up at my apartment with a stack of campaign flyers in the backseat that we never passed out and we complemented one another on our dresses. I had just spent the last fifteen minutes pacing upstairs in my apartment as I rehearsed that sixty-second speech we were allotted before the vote.

"I like Mike" and "I like Susan" were standing at the doors with their team, which included a curly-haired six-year-old in a bow tie, greeting the delegates with campaign stickers and handouts. Kelly and

I passed through them with our heads down wishing we perhaps tried harder. The line for registration was long, and the atrium of the elementary school was buzzing. The halls were lined with promotion tables touting Trump, Young Republicans, the National Committee Woman incumbent, and the like. As we waited—wearing our competition's stickers—Kelly surveyed the crowd and anxiously admitted,

"I don't think I want to do this! I think I'm going to take my name off the slate." I encouraged her not to, but her nerves were more convincing. She found the secretary for the convention and asked to have her name removed from consideration. *Well, if she wasn't running, why should I?* I asked myself as my nerves strengthened. Recollecting what brought me there that day, I laughed as the oddities added up. I resisted many of the Lord's attempts to lead me there, and sure enough, he still managed to put me in line that day, and I realized that I had to follow through on my end—it was clear he wanted me there.

Kelly and I found our seats which were reserved for Young Republican delegates and alternate delegates, located next to the senior citizen delegates at the top row of the theater auditorium. We sat patiently throughout the animated discussion of convention rules and our congressional district platform. A few hours later, the chair of the convention called the candidates for national delegates to the foot of the stage to line up alphabetically and give our speeches. I waited behind a Maddox and in front of a Lund as my legs quivered, betraying my confidence. Maddox was a war veteran who described his fight for our freedom and I felt bad for what I was about to do—rock it. When they called out my name, I grabbed the mic and took the only breath time allowed me. I began my plea for their support and asked if my vision was theirs too. I guess it was. On the second ballot, I felt it. It had to happen. It did—they picked me.

THE BACHELOR

Josh, a new Asian friend who found humor in his white-boy personality, brought us to his delegation's ice cream social for Iowan Senator Chuck Grassley. Having worked in Iowa the previous summer, I was familiar with this U.S. Senator though was not fortunate enough to have met him. Kelly, Jeremiah, and Robert (the Minnesotans) jumped at the opportunity for free ice cream and a meet-and-greet with Senator Grassley. I went along, always excited about free food. As our Uber took us further out of the city of Cleveland and the streets became littered and the pedestrians were rougher-looking, we worried Josh was taking us on an unwanted detour. Before we became too concerned and asked the driver to bring us back downtown, we came upon an eclectic avenue of restaurants and shops, and, thankfully, the ice cream shop we were looking for. We passed the security detail of six outside the doors and were shown upstairs to the event. The room was crowded with Iowan farmers (and people with jobs in the few other industries Iowa has) and a sprinkling of really attractive young men. A young woman approached our out-of-place-looking group as we stood in the middle of the rows of tables, looking around, and she took our ice cream orders. A table cleared in time for us to sit and eat just before the Senator was introduced. I didn't hear much of what he had to say because I was focused on not eating ice cream like a pig in front of anyone who might be paying attention—particularly the good-looking sirs behind me. I clearly needed to be reminded that no one cares about the way I spoon ice cream into my mouth.

"Claire! Claire!" Kelly shouted in a whisper across the table as our speaker continued. I turned over my right shoulder, providing her my attention.

"That's the Bachelor! Chris Soules!!" She quietly exclaimed with her thumb pointed toward who stood behind her.

I casually raised my eyes above her head and noticed a model dressed in blue. His beard reflected his perfect age—older and within the acceptable dating range, and his posture proclaimed a self-assurance that made him even more attractive. My eyes delighted in the sight. Kelly continued with her fan-girl moment, taking noticeable selfies with him in the background; any attractive person is observant enough to know when someone's taking a picture of them. I laughed with indifference to this run-in with a Bachelor.

As the audience demonstrated their amusement with the speaker, Kelly, being the great wing-woman that she was, said,

"Claire, you should go talk to Chris!"

"No, thanks." I didn't watch his season. He was cute, but he was practically a celebrity and one that wouldn't have any interest in me or whatever awkward thing I'd have to say.

"I really think you should! Do you want a picture with him?"

I continued to pass on her suggestions.

We stood around, talking with the Iowan Speaker of the House whom Josh knew and waited for the boys to get their photo taken with the Senator. I kept an eye on Chris's encounters (though I wasn't a fan, he was still a celebrity) and Kelly kept pushing for a picture. Kelly was watching Chris and former Governor Rick Santorum take a picture with a few people, and decided she wanted one herself. I encouraged her to get one and offered to take the picture. I snapped a few photos of her with the former Bachelor and Governor—an odd combination. As she left the embrace of the two gentlemen, Kelly asked if I wanted a picture. Embarrassed to be just popping in for a picture but humble enough to recognize the insult of denying my interest in a picture with either them, I agreed and stepped in between these two personalities. As I turned around to get into position, Chris prodded excitedly with a smile (at least, that's what it looked like to me),

"Wait, what's your name?" I told him and asked for his though I can't recall if I had forgotten it or if I quickly discerned that it would be a natural thing to ask for. We smiled for the picture, and my brain began to sweep the room for how to initiate a conversation.

I was beginning to learn that being awkward is okay. Many coworkers and friends might be surprised that I was only then accepting this when I have been awkward for years, but when it comes to romantic endeavors, I've accepted that there are going to be a lot of awkward situations that I'm going to have to sit in, to feel, and to accept that it's okay and to just move on.

So, there I was walking out of the embrace, looking for a place to start.

"So you're from Iowa then?" I asked, my head spinning.

"Yup," he offered with his soft, breathy voice.

I began to mumble something about being from Minnesota and bailed, jumping into the one other thing I knew about him.

"So my friend told me you were on the Bachelor. Is that right?"

"Yeah, yup I was—"

"That must've been quite the experience? What was your favorite thing about being a part of that?"

He mumbled on about his experience, and I inquired about a few more things before retiring that subject. I asked him what he did for a living (later finding out this was a revealing question because it demonstrated that I truly never did see his show and didn't know who he was—this being a plus for a Bachelor trying to find an honest wife). He described his passion for farming, its importance, and the value of family. I shared my experience in Iowa the previous summer, my appreciation for it, and my interest in farming (again, later learning that his Bachelor-show engagement ended because his fiancé wasn't willing to move to Iowa for him). Five or ten minutes later, a friend waved to him as he was leaving, awakening me to the surroundings to see that they were kicking everyone out. Wanting to end the conversation first to maintain my newfound fangirl dignity, I interjected,

"Oops, looks like they're kicking us out—"

"Yeah, yeah—"

"I've got to go meet up with my friends. It was really nice meeting you."

"Yeah, see you around?"

"Hopefully!" I admitted smiling, slowly leaving his side with a prayer that he'd stop me to ask for my number. But he didn't.

I continued down the stairs with my posse making light conversation while my head continued to spin over my encounter with one of America's most eligible Bachelors. As we stepped outside to wait for our Uber, Kelly begged for details then stopped me when I started—

"Did he ask for your number?!"

"No," I admitted scrunching my face.

"Give me your business card. I'll run in and give it to him!" I paused trying to avoid desperation but quickly gave in, dug out one of my cards and handed it off like a relay race and awaited his call that never came.

It isn't surprising when I look back on it—the chances that this TV star would, within minutes, fall for a naive girl who overestimated her looks and ate cookies for breakfast. But for a few days, I practiced hope in what many would see as the impossible. Of course, I didn't see it that way—I always believed God makes crazy things happen, and this could very well have been one of them. Still, it wasn't, which must mean there's something even better coming.

GRANDMA

This had happened before. Once again, I received a call from my dad suggesting that I visit Grandma because she took a "turn for the worse"—a phrase that no longer alarmed me. Perhaps it was the frequency in which I responded to such news or maybe it was because I had anticipated this time for the past three wheelchair-bound years of her life, or perhaps it was the peace in knowing her time had finally come.

I loved my grandma more than my tears could fill a rain gauge, and for years, I would sit in the La-Z-Boy next to Grandma in her rocking chair as we watched *Everybody Loves Raymond*—her with a re-heated cup of black coffee and a Sandy cookie and I with my Diet Coke and soda-fountain glass of cookies-and-cream ice cream. I would revel in that moment. She was sure to reach her end faster than the rest of us, and I reminded myself of that every day.

My fondest memories of her were her days at the fifty-five-plus Senior Living apartment complex on Douglas Drive in Crystal, MN. Those were the fullest years of my time with her. As a family, we would hop into the maroon soccer van on a Friday night to head to Grandma's where we would order pizza and go swimming. We would play the only card game her memory could muscle, Skip-bo, and in the earlier years we'd toss the battery-operated Hot Potato. Her refrigerator was never absent of Sour Cream and Onion potato chip dip, and their pairing always sat atop the fridge with a potato chip clip. Half-sized Diet Coke cans and water bottles lined a shelf next to the hot dogs which were a permanent part of her diet. Half of the half-order of the Applebee's Oriental Chicken Salad usually found its way into her refrigerator alongside another leftover from lunch with her girlfriends the day before. Her freezer always kept vanilla and cookies-and-cream ice cream cold, and in her later years, she added single-serving chocolate-vanilla ice cream cups to the mix.

If we weren't coming to visit, we were coming to pick her up for church or one of the grandkids' sporting games or a school play. She would wait outside with her purse secured on the front side of her hip, its strap around the other shoulder, and one hand on the railing and the other on her bronze cane. She stood with great patience, her knees slightly bent. Grandma volunteered as an "I'm Okay" walker—a resident who would walk around her floor to flip the door hangers on the doors of residents who signaled they were upright for the day, and if Grandma came upon a door that was missing a hanger, she would call for help—but didn't do enough walking to keep her strong through her final days. I can't blame her for not working harder to keep her body able; I don't know how hard it is to get old.

Towards the end of her stay at the Heathers, I was in college in St. Paul with a favorable class schedule so I spent Friday mornings and afternoons with Grandma. I would take her to an early lunch, usually at Applebee's or the Crystal Cafe up the road where we got to know the waitresses and had a standard order. We would stop on the way home at the bank—because as my father joked, her printing press in her apartment was broken—or Almsted's for more frozen lasagna dinners, cookies, and toiletries. She would walk slowly as she held on tight to the cart for stability. She would usually that I pick out something for myself. After I dropped her at the door and carried in her purchases, I would sit with her for another hour or so. Often I would wash her hair over the kitchen sink, then dry and curl it to the tune of *Everybody Loves Raymond* or maybe a Twins Game. We would each have our Diet Cokes next to us, and she would share stories of her earlier years. I would then take care of anything she needed doing around her apartment, mostly taking out the trash or recycling on my way out.

I recall these times I spent with my grandma, and every prior time she came to a game with a blue cooler filled with pop and snacks, or would take us kids to Dairy Queen after School Mass on Fridays, or would be present at every birthday and celebration, as my fortune. I was blessed with so much time to be with her and knew that time would cease.

Driving with the windows down in my air-conditioned-less car, I impatiently headed towards St. Therese, Grandma's home for her last three years. Those years were some of the hardest. Thanksgiving in 2014, about a year after she moved into her new apartment, my Dad was having trouble getting ahold of my grandma by phone, so he dropped by. After some obstacles, he entered her apartment to find her lying on the ground next to her rocking chair. The in-house doctors came to assess her condition; her heart-rate was inconsistent and aside from a bruised eye, they said she would be okay, but she was never the same.

The following day, I went to visit her with my dad. She was sleeping as expected. My dad tried to communicate with her, but she couldn't comprehend and communicate in return. He asked me to stay with her while he ran out. I didn't know what good I would do sitting there while she slept, what to be concerned about while she slept or when she woke, or what to do if I noticed something, but I agreed with the hope that my dad would return quickly. He returned a few hours later and immediately went in to check on Grandma. She began to stir. My dad wisely checked the bed to see if she had wet the bed; she had. Concerned for her health, he ordered me to take the sheets and throw them in the wash while he helped her into the bathroom. I watched her hero practically carry her to the bathroom and help her undress from the urine soaked clothes and got her to the toilet. I was in awe watching this son care for his mother and tried to help as best my body could as it grounded chills that involuntarily arose. Shortly after, she was admitted to the hospital to address her inconsistent heart rate. A few days later they sent her home, only to receive her again a week later. Her heart apnea was not resolved, and the doctors told us this would likely continue—home to hospital to home to hospital. I remember sitting on the floor with my mom and dad in our living room that Christmas learning of this predicament, and the looming decision that had to be made: do we just let it run its course at home or continue this trauma? Remorseful over life's cruel burden thrust upon our family—choosing life or death for our loved one—I broke down in tears before my parents.

The sadness penetrated my limbs, rendering them useless to do anything but wipe the tears that would otherwise soak my t-shirt.

Thankfully, by the time we needed to make that heart-wrenching decision she overcame the dark prognosis from the doctor, and her heart began to cope on its own. Yet, it was not strong enough to return her to her better years. She was moved into Transitional Care while she stabilized and then into Long-Term Care where she remained in a single room with a few portraits and keepsakes for her remaining days.

Such days were filled with complaints of the food, accusations of the staff being rough with her and the lack of daily activity. Yet, these days were also filled with laughter and joy. She would smile, she was curious, she was a Twins fan, she was witty, she could still enjoy life's simple pleasures. In those last few years, my parents honored her through their constant attention and outpouring of love. And Grandma found ways to return it: in her excitement when we walked through the door, in her BINGO prizes she shared, in her quirky remarks, and in her laughter. Yes, there was still much goodness in her life.

I didn't know what to expect when I walked into her Long-Term Care room that Thursday evening. My heart had not softened yet to consider the pending reality. My family had been with her for most of the evening, and I received a general report of the situation and was advised to say my goodbyes. She was so thin, her deep-wrinkled cheeks concaving. Her jaw hung open which lacked her Parkinson's shake. The rest of her body was likewise still, while her artery tried to escape through her neck. Her breathing deepened and quickened, then would subside for nearly too long. I sat on the side of the bed and spoke to her with the only words I could gather: I love you, Grandma, so much. When the room had cleared, I leaned forward to embrace her weak body. I could only rest my body on top of hers. I wept on her shoulder. I whispered my heart in her ear. I didn't know how goodbyes were supposed to go.

Throughout the next week, family cycled through the room; my dad and aunt Cheryl alternated night shifts to ensure Grandma always had someone with her. After five days in the same state, we began trying methods to help her let go—telling her of who and what was waiting for her, affirming her with our love and support, giving her time alone to pass.

On day seven, my aunt Cheryl sat up during the night going through her mom's things in the room, throwing away old greeting cards and setting things aside to save. She found a stack of letters her brother John had written to their mom when he was in the Navy. The letters were casual—detailing his days—and loving. He did love his mom; that was real, despite the years he left her alone with only the memory of his hurtful goodbye. Within minutes, Grandma stopped breathing. Perhaps she had finally received the closure she had been holding on for. I woke to a text and breathed my last with her on this earth.

A LONG ROAD TO A FENCE

We flew from Minneapolis to Las Vegas on a Friday night at 9:00 p.m. Our parents took us to the airport, and as usual, parked and went inside with us until we passed through security—which surprisingly with my Swiss Army Knife keychain and Alex's quart-size bag filled with alcoholic shooters, we made it through quickly and painlessly. Between the other travelers and metal detectors, we waved goodbye to them, having agreed we would be in contact again once we landed and once again when we made it to our destination that night.

Around 11:00 p.m. my brother and I landed in Las Vegas with our one personal item allotted to us by Spirit Airlines and took the bus to the airport's rental car area. We checked-in and were given the option of a white compact Fiat or its competition, a bright red Toyota compact. We both eagerly agreed to the Fiat, signed the agreement I failed to read diligently, and settled into the two-door vehicle that might have needed to double as our lodging that night.

Being the city that never sleeps, we found a twenty-four-hour Walmart nearby, surrounded by palm trees and warm air that surely reminded us we were far from the Midwestern conifers and colorful maples that we left behind. We entered the superstore with a general list of must-haves: sleeping bags, air mattress, firewood, and food.

Knowing our shelter was most important that night, we headed straight to the back for camping gear. Perusing the shelves, we picked out the cheapest sleeping bag and quickly realized the air-mattress-pump was an extra expense we hadn't considered and opted for two two-dollar tarps to lay on the ground. I was unsure of the purpose of a tarp in this case but had read during my Google searches of "Can I just put a sleeping bag down in the desert and sleep?" that people usually put tarps down first. It couldn't have been for comfort, and if it was because of rodents or bugs, surely they could traverse a tarp to reach me and eat me alive, but I followed the crowd and we threw the blue tarps into the cart. Speaking of bugs, were there mosquitos in the desert? We asked a guy looking at fishing gear in the next aisle. He said we didn't need to worry about mosquitos or other flying bugs, and after living in the area for thirty-some years, he had seen a scorpion only once and said we should primarily be on the lookout for something he had no name for and that was relatively harmless. I tried to ignore that last part, as I was still uneasy about sleeping openly in the desert.

We added firewood, a lighter, flashlights (which we never used), and binoculars to the cart. We spent longer on deciding what alcohol to purchase than what binoculars to buy since we couldn't keep anything cold on the two-hour drive to Area 51 and had to drink whatever we purchased before flying home in twenty-four hours. We ended up getting Diet Coke and a case of water and picked up a bottle of spiced Captain Morgan on our way out of town. Alex added hotdogs and Red Bull, and I grabbed a Monster energy drink. I had already been awake for twenty hours, and we still had a whole night ahead of us; I was unsure if one energy drink would be enough.

By 1:00 a.m., we had exhausted our shopping and began our journey north. The city lights shone magnificently in our rearview mirror. Our parents had taken us to the same city ten years prior, but it looked different this time. This time, it was only part of the backdrop, not our main destination. We watched it fade into the background as the mountains began to rise around us. We admired the full moon and its reflection of the sun which cast a dim glow upon the mountains that rose and fell along the length of Highway 93. *AM Coast-to-Coast*, the nationally syndicated call-in talk show catering to the freaky—the paranormal, the extraterrestrial, the unexplained, and the questions that drive conspiracy theories—came through the radio. We listened to the callers as we kept an eye on the car behind us that had been following us since we turned off Interstate 15. The missing head-light suggested it might not be a government vehicle tracking us, but who was it then? We didn't know who was behind us or what was before us.

The desert was bright, casting light upon the dwarf bushes and various desert trees that salted the valley between the cascading mountains. We saw maybe three or four cars during our drive north. After turning onto the Extraterrestrial Highway, we stopped to assess the highway sign that had been plastered with bumper stickers by other travelers searching for whatever they might find near the highly secretive air force base. The one-headlight SUV continued on, and we were really alone now. The anticipation was building. Without a destination in mind, we continued down the highway. The landscape became more complex, bending the roads into curves and hills. We had to be on the lookout for the free-range cattle or wildlife that could halt our small car. I also had my eye on the gas gauge as we passed a sign warning us of the hundred-mile distance to the next gas station. I crossed my fingers. The reality of the adventure we were on set in and uneasiness drifted through my bones. Within minutes, we passed a rock that sat as if it was placed so intentionally, with graffiti so disconcerting as to dissuade sojourners from proceeding any further. We slowed to a stop and turned the car around to take a closer look. The art appeared to say, "Go Back." I looked around, assessing the situation. The moon was favorable lighting to see the outlines of our surroundings. Rocks rose high next to the road creating more shadows than my stomach could handle. A small dirt road split from the highway about fifty feet behind us. There was no signage noting an address if it was a registered home or business, and the road had no discernible end. Already apprehensive to continue down the marked road, I could not muster the courage to follow the unmarked one as Alex playfully suggested, and I insisted we continue onward.

We kept our eyes peeled for a reasonable place to stop and rest for the night, but every widened shoulder was only big enough for an emergency stop. So, we continued, both agreeing that the less time we had our sleeping bags rolled out, the less vulnerable we would be to wild animals, or worse—crazy locals. Eventually, we saw a few distant lights from the homes of Rachel residents. The town of fifty-four required few establishments, but the Little A'Le'Inn we had read so much about prior to our visit sat clearly on the left-hand side of the road. We slowly pulled into the parking lot and stopped in front of its bright sign that welcomed earthlings. Venturing around the gravel parking lot, we studied the area. The motel included a series of trailer homes set to the West of the restaurant. Likely the only fire truck within a 100-miles radius was tucked behind a fence just south of the establishment and what I assumed to be the owner's home sat parallel to the restaurant just south of the fire truck. Our feet were loud upon the pebbles as we tried not to disrupt the campers who slept in the open lot to the east. A motorhome, small car, and truck with a retro, metal trailer were parked a few hundred feet apart from one another, and Alex and I decided our best option for the night was to stay near them in case we ran into trouble— like alien trouble. We returned to the car and drove it into the open lot that spanned perhaps a half square mile and spawned small desert plants upon its pebbly soil.

At that point, around 4:00 a.m., we opened the trunk of the car and set out our luxuries. One tarp served as a seat for the fire that Alex began building. The Captain Diets were poured into five-cent styrofoam cups, and I indulged on a "late night" snack of Cheez-its. Alex lamented of his ignorance in assuming he could find a stick in the desert with which to cook his hot dog and ended up setting it on a piece of firewood to roast. The air was cool. We zipped-up and huddled close to the fire. I was still nervous to lay down and let the wild watch me sleep, so I enjoyed the activity at hand, every so often checking the ground around me to see if any creepy-crawlers had come out to join us. We chatted with the car trunk to our back, watching the fire and stars to the East— the lot stretching vastly before us. Conversation spanned the spectrum and time passed without bore or tiredness. We had been up for twenty-four hours, but being in the desert so close to secrecy and the source of stories that have been extrapolated and promulgated for seventy-years was all too energizing. I thought about deploying those communication techniques some documentaries have explored, and quickly realized I wasn't prepared for whatever encounter could come from that. So, I just conversed with my brother in the free and timeless way one does when they are remote and grounded in the universe.

Yes, Alex and I had come a long way—sure, to Las Vegas, but together, as siblings. It was a few months back that in our normal way we were sitting in our living room like strangers with my parents. I was telling my parents of my interest in taking a trip to Area 51 and Alex offered to go with me. In my eagerness to go, I agreed to his offer, figuring I was desperate for someone crazy enough to make the trip with and we didn't necessarily have to talk. But we did. More astonishingly, he did. He talked about his life, feelings, and opinions, and asked me about the same. The past few years had worn on my openness towards him, and I could sense that hesitancy still, but he was open—and chatty. So much of the time I listened, accepting his offering, grateful he was crazy enough to be there with me.

Entranced by the glow of the fire, my eyes would free themselves occasionally to scan the skies and admire its characteristics that often go unnoticed in the city. I detected a bright light that was redder and bigger than, but still comparable to, a star. As Alex followed my extended finger into the cluster of stars, he disagreed that it might be Mars, suggesting it was a plane because it was not stationary. I took another look. As we continued our gaze, it began moving and moving fast. Without taking my eyes off it for fear I'd lose it, I nudged my brother: "Did you see that?!" We both watched eagerly trying to piece together our observations into some reasonable explanation. It darted horizontally to the right then stopped. It then began zig-zagging upward and dashed diagonally to the left. A plane could not change directions like that; it was too high to be a helicopter or drone; it was in the opposite direction of the air force base. This was most likely not what they would want us to believe. This was a UFO by definition. At one point, I thought I discerned it drawing nearer, close enough that I grabbed the keys and had one leg in the car ready to bolt. It retreated, and I went back to my observation post by the fire. We watched it dart throughout the Southeastern sky for over thirty minutes. It remained still at times and other times, unsteady. It was a marvelous mystery.

Eventually, the foreign object became mundane, and our eyes became heavy. By 6:00 a.m. we rolled out our sleeping bags onto the tarp, extinguished the fire, and nuzzled into our polyester cocoons. But I couldn't sleep knowing the UFO was still buzzing nearby—I backed myself up against Alex's body which somehow fell fast asleep, and kept my ears alert for any concerning sounds. As my body drifted to sleep, I heard a dog barking in the distance and the sound effects from *The X-Files*. Figuring any extra-terrestrial could do their deed to me in Minneapolis just as easily as there in the desert, I just let the sounds of my imagination feed my imagination and surrendered to sleep.

I awoke and poked my head out of the little hole I left for air at the top of my bag. The crisp morning air brushed against my face and the morning sun touched the surface of my skin. The air smelled of earth, and the desert expanded around me. I put my glasses on and could finally see the extent of the mountain range in the distance and the few homes that were scattered along its base. I continued to inhale the crisp freshness of dawn, reveling in the desert's wonder.

By 8:30 a.m., I had softly kicked Alex enough to wake him, and we rose from our sleeping bags to begin packing up camp. Our schedule was flexible and relatively without much expectation, so we took our time. We snacked on the remaining Cheez-its and poured another Captain Diet as the other campers stirred about their vehicles. The Little A'Le'Inn was a hive of activity with visitors coming and going so early on that Saturday morning. Alex and I eventually made our way into the restaurant to explore the gift shop. We spent too long studying the trinkets, shirts, and themed glassware that lined the restaurant walls. Seeing us mill about, the owner, Pat, asked us if we needed help with anything. We declined her offer and eventually purchased fifty dollars worth of souvenirs—well, Alex did, I opted for a five-dollar "Area 51" shot glass that I'll never use. Eager to share our experience but embarrassed to be so forthcoming about it, I approached the owner again:

"I bet you hear a lot of stories about what people see around here," I said trying to be coy about the information I held. Standing across from her where she sat at a round table with an employee who was eating breakfast on break.

"Oh, yeah, there's always something," she responded like she already wasn't going to believe me.

"Yeah, we saw something too last night. It was a reddish light in the sky that darted about for half-an-hour in ways I've never seen before. What do you think that could have been?" I asked, avoiding sharing my own conclusions. She casually chalked it up to testing by the Air Force though I wondered why the Air Force would use air space outside of the base when I thought the whole purpose of the base was for testing. I didn't push any theories with her but offered a "Huh..." displaying my consideration of her response and went on to share our great experience in her town.

We meandered outside to look around the restaurant in daylight. We spoke with some locals who sat near an informational mining plaque we had approached to read. A weathered man elaborated on the trips he would take through the desert and how he would always stop to visit his friends in Rachel. Pat came outside with a wireless landline in her hand.

"I think your mom's on the phone," she said to us with a smirk. Alex and I turned to her in great confusion as the locals chuckled. I paused.

"Is her name Becky?" I asked trying to verify whether the call was really for us. Pat replied confidently,

"It's your mom."

I took the phone from her.

"This is Claire."

"Claire! Thank God, I've been worried sick!" She lamented over the past five hours of torture not hearing from us. I explained that we didn't have cell phone service and we're doing just fine. I remorsefully calmed her nerves, still shocked that she had reached us through the phone of a restaurant in the middle of the desert.

Mom was okay, our souvenir itch was satisfied, and our classic chat with the locals had ended, and we squeezed back into the Fiat and opened the map Alex had purchased for fifty cents inside. The map was really just a drawing of the roads that led to the back gate of Area 51 with a series of warnings that essentially said: don't be an idiot. Though dramatic and restrictive, we found it equally helpful in navigating the journey alone that had led our foregoers to imprisonment and, in my wild imagination, death. Estimating the miles eastward, we looked for a dirt road to our right. The black mailbox signaled our turn. The mailbox belongs to a resident of the area, but Area 51 enthusiasts revere it as a symbol of secrecy. A second mailbox was added for interspace mail because the resident tired of receiving outgoing mail to aliens.

Alex and I continued down the dirt road without stopping to mail our postcards to ETs—our gas gauge was too low to consider unnecessary pit stops. We channeled the 1990s to follow the map without help from a GPS. A green homemade "51" sign directed us to keep going. The dust swirled behind us as the compact moved freely about the dirt road, unable to stay in one car track. I gripped the wheel tighter as if it could give us better gas mileage and watched the estimate dip from twenty-eight miles per gallon to twenty-three miles per gallon to nineteen miles per gallon. I knew we couldn't travel seventeen hundred miles only to turn around for gas. For my own sanity, I told Alex that it would be no big deal if we ran out of gas; we'd simply walk and get more—walk forty-some miles and back. I kept my hands tight on the wheel and pressed on.

We flew over one hill, then another, and swerved around a corner and saw the gate. Well, it was two signs on either side of the road. The signs forbade the use of drones or cameras, even though our Little A'Le'Inn official map gave us permission for pictures. Alex dug out our twenty-dollar binoculars, and we studied the area. The gate was placed snuggly between two hills covered in bushes and sprinkled with trees. We searched the trees in hopes to catch a glimpse of snipers or hidden equipment. Some equipment they didn't hide, including cameras, radar, and sensors. Barbed wire lined the border and the "camo dudes" sat alert in their white pick-up truck at the top of the hill just behind the installation. Engines hummed in the distance behind the low mountain range ahead. We were so close to, and so separated from, the truth. Then we got back in our car and headed home for the experience to live on in memory.

It lives vibrantly in my memory. It spanned a mere twenty-four hours, and still, my heart excites in wonderment of the adventure. Perhaps it spoke to my simple soul. Perhaps it spoke of a mystery.

We searched for something hidden and laid to rest without comforts. We turned out the lights and looked towards the sky. We handed ourselves over to the mercy of the road and opened our hearts to whatever we would find. It's as if I caught a glimpse of how fulfilling our lives can be when we seek, by a simple way, the glory of creation possessing no more than we need with only the road to guide our way.

Chapter Six

Crystallization

KNOCKING

I hadn't seen her for a year. This old friend, the best one during my formative high school years, entered my life once again through the church community we shared. We met for dinner, something we hadn't done since our adolescent, boyfriend-less years. We caught up between mouthfuls of bar food where she told me about her first year of marriage, and I shared with her the dreaded phone conversation that was scheduled later that night with a guy I decided not to date anymore. Amongst these relationship discussions, I joked, as I often did in the depths of my struggle to find a man to whom I was eager to commit to, that if I'm still single by the time I'm thirty-years-old, I'll just join the religious sisterhood.

Kristen laughed then continued with sincerity inquiring about my discernment. Ashamed, I didn't feel I could properly respond without having properly discerned. My discernment had always been just a feeling from a fleeting thought. Sometimes, though, it wouldn't flee so swiftly, and I'd catch it. When I did, I would recall my need to pray thoughtfully about this option and to act. A week later, the match would burn out, and I'd be back stalking new love interests on Facebook. So, I admitted to Kristen that I hadn't discerned my vocation and saw my need to resolve conflicting desires, or more sufficiently, my need to abandon myself to our Lord's will.

Kristen shared that within her first year of marriage, she doubted she was living the right vocation, scared of the life she chose. Kristen talked to her friends who had led her through her discernment of marriage; they reminded her that she had discerned the Lord's will, that she had prayed thoughtfully and was guided into marriage, and that this was the work of Satan who wanted to separate what God had brought together. It was then I realized my foolishness. I'd left the Lord standing outside my door for eight years. I'd heard his knock and walked towards the door, but the TV was loud and I went to turn it down and got hooked on it again. I kept allowing myself to ignore the man at my door who wanted to talk. I realized my foolishness and couldn't ignore him any longer.

A week later, driving to the adoration chapel to spend some face-to-face time with God and take another step towards discernment, tears streamed down my face as I considered this potential request of his—to be his. Like a beloved, I pondered what my life would look like with him. The bright lights that approached me in the darkness glowed through the lens of my welling eyes. *Oh, what happiness might truly look like,* I thought. I surveyed this imagined storyline to assess its emotion. *Is this sadness?* For I could also see my once assumed life slipping through my fingers, never begotten. The once possessed, my worldly identity, washed away. Though I saw my foolishness and call it meaningless when I face the reality of the truly satisfying, my heart still feared to let the world go. My heart feared many things.

My heart even feared the Lord's will. As I thought about my strengths, abilities, and talents, I wondered how they fit into the lifestyle of a sister or if they could even be used and where. When I thought about the people in my life who've shaped and loved me, I wondered how I could leave them. I considered my adoring parents who received so much joy from watching, and partaking in, my life, and wondered how I could take that away from them. I thought about the family and children that would never be known to me or the world. I considered the abandonment of possessions and the relinquishment of my given name—the name I came to love so many years ago.

And still, I love the Lord's will. I know it is only for my good. I know it is his drawing of his beloved. He only asks for my love, and in my love, I choose him and whatever consequence may follow. I glimpse joy. I am overwhelmed by its sight. I both recognize the sacrifice—the self-giving—in married life and likewise in the sisterhood. I am called to one over the other, however beautiful the other may be, and however worthy of the making of a saint.

Perhaps this desire was merely to pull me into spiritual growth to prepare me for marriage, or perhaps too, it was indeed to prepare me for the consecrated life—the very life of so many saints.

Sister Faustina, the Carmelite I contacted expressing interest in her Come and See retreat, recommended, amidst my rambling of a brief biography serving to acquaint her with my spiritual history, that I read St. Therese of Lisieux's autobiography, *The Story of a Soul*.

Her story unfolded a beautiful account of God's beloved, and though I often felt through her story a lesser desire for the sisterhood, I felt more deeply inspired to love through her little way and glimpse the fullness of the glory of God. She drew me closer to him. I wanted to find him in the same places as she did, and speak to him in the same child-like, endless-loving way. As I came to the end of her story, she spoke of flowers in a way that drew something familiar out of me. I thought I might have prayed to her before; perhaps it was a novena. And upon my brief internet search, I found the very same page that I had referenced, even bookmarked, as a novena to ask for a husband. Now, clearly, those prayers were not answered in the way I had hoped. I could understand why—I wouldn't want to have met my husband already; there were many things I wouldn't have experienced and grown in if I had. I first prayed to her by recommendation of someone eight years ago. St. Therese was a Carmelite; I unknowingly pursued the same order in my discernment as she so rightfully lived, which led me to her autobiography, which put me on my couch at 9:00 p.m. in the middle of the week putting the pieces together. Suddenly, I felt so close to the Lord's Little Flower, that she had wanted to be my friend all along. Having gotten to know her through her own words, having grown in confidence in this Saint's promise to spend her heaven doing good on earth, I turned to her once again, at the heart of my discernment, asking for her to draw out the Lord's perfect will and shower me with flowers. I asked her to *shower* me, to pour them over me—red ones if the Lord invites me to the consecrated life, and white ones if the Lord wills for me to become a saint through marriage. After I had begun the novena, I felt joy depart and was left slightly disappointed, for I think I trusted in St. Therese's intercession so greatly that I believed after the succeeding nine days, my discernment would end and I would know, with certainty, the Lord's will. Throughout the last month, my flame had been fed the oxygen to grow and burn brighter. I had felt consumed by love, hopeful in its infinite presence. I feared that in nine days, all would be settled and my spiritual growth would cease. So, part way through the novena I added a request for pink flowers in case the Lord wished not to disclose his precious word yet but St. Therese still wanted to affirm her friendship with me.

Certainly, I recognized the journey towards sainthood and the unraveling of God's will as a lifelong pursuit, and I delighted in that course (even though she didn't give me flowers this time), so I packed my overnight bag for a Come and See retreat a few months later.

I arrived with great indifference. Perhaps it was the shock from the end of a gruesome political campaign season, the stress of beginning a new career in sales, or the decision of my vocation that laid before me which left my heart so worn and pulled that weekend. But the religious sisters were expecting me, and with my less-than-prepared heart, I brought myself to that suburban church with the most conservative clothes I owned and a journal I hoped would be my refuge. My mind was open to the potential of what the Lord would reveal to me through the retreat, but how did I know if my heart was? I had come as I was, trusting the Lord would use what I brought him.

The weekend dragged on with lectures, communal meals, and the Divine Office. My prayer was vacant, and my heart was heavy. From what, I couldn't tell. Friday night, I climbed into my sleeping bag on the floor surrounded by twelve other young women in the basement music room and rested with questions. As my heart grew in pain, I thought I should leave, just go. Nothing was holding me there. I didn't need to ask permission. I could just leave—this wasn't for me. The discomfort informed me this was not what I was called to. The anxiety worsened, and I forced myself to breathe steadily and fully. Perhaps it was the shame of leaving that kept me there that night—fearing I would look like I'm running away from something—or perhaps it was truly my desire for a retreat regardless of the kind, but, likely, it was the grace of God that urged me on, and I woke the next morning at 6:00 a.m. next to the other young women who might have been battling the evil one too.

The heaviness remained, and my distractions worsened. I wondered if the sisters could sense my discomfort or withdrawal. I was trying to meet the Lord there, and I knew he was reaching out, but I couldn't sense him. I asked Sister Bridgette for her advice—we sat at one of the round tables in the adjoining gym Sunday morning, her brown, habited lap held the handmade rosary that hung from her side and she listened to my challenges of the weekend. This woman in her sixties with the wits of her age but the joy of a little girl reminded me that Satan, too, was working that weekend. When Satan sees someone growing closer to the Lord, he does everything he can to stop them. The sisters called these works scallops, like when a multitude of dishes break at their home when they're welcoming a new group of ladies into their religious order. Satan actively works against holiness, she reminded me, and that the Lord only speaks through peace. This discomfort was not coming from the Lord.

So, I was left to discern what Satan was trying to keep me from. Was it hearing my vocation to the religious life? Was it hearing my vocation at all? Too, he could have simply been keeping me from the Lord himself. Though I walked out of those church doors Sunday afternoon with a stronger assessment of the desire that had led me there—that my draw towards the sisterhood with its rules, discipline, service, and focus on the Lord was spiritually immature and not that of a true calling, I don't think I heard the Lord. So, I took this back to my spiritual director, and the journey of discernment continued.

A GREAT HOLE

I sat in the first pew to the right of the altar as Father stood at the podium speaking about the happy couple. He spoke of my friends' witness to the truth, of their great love for God and one another, and their choice in selecting Tobit 8:4-8 to be read during their wedding Mass. Father spoke of Tobiah's prayer that showered heaven with thanks and his plea for mercy, a prayer for him and his new wife, a prayer we, too, should lift up in our marriages. Surely, by the grace of God, my hope was renewed in the beauty of marriage and its great capacity for holiness. My heart overflowed with great joy for my friends and in what, too, might be delivered to me.

The man I've seen in my dreams sat towards the back of the church hearing those same words of Father's and I wondered if he was wondering about me too. I had never met a man who was both expressive of his love for the Lord and a man to whom I was so attracted. As Father's words sank in, I reveled in the potential of what could become of me, and what could become of him. As the ceremony ended and we enjoyed the evening's festivities, we often found our way back to one another from our respective spots on the dance floor with other prospective partners. My wing-woman, Courtney, talked me up to him mercilessly, and by the end of the night, he had confided that I was marriage material—a woman he could list nine alluring qualities of after six hours with her—but one he wasn't mature enough to pursue. My hope extinguished; my heart broke. It seems dramatic to express the emotion as such, but neither *disappointment* nor *hurt* could substantiate the pit in my stomach that was steadily growing.

I awoke the next morning from the reverberations of the depression that was made in my heart from the hope that had been renewed and revoked over the course of hours. Here was finally a man I rightfully desired, and I would never see him again. Throughout the day, whenever my mind would drift to the night before, the same feeling would arise. I wondered what this meant. Certainly, as the Lord is faithful, he could use this to speak to me—so what was he telling me about the vocation he has placed on my heart?

At this point, I do not know. Perhaps it was a demonstration of my reliance on man to satisfy the needs of my heart. Surely, man could never match the commitment of Our Lord. Or, in my current state and limit in understanding, perhaps the Lord was showing me my greatest desire, one I didn't know I had, a desire he put on my heart for a holy son of His who would one day become my spouse.

So here, I fear, I start from scratch.

A New Beginning

Alas, the years had been what they needed to be. In irony, I attempt to account for them in words when words only followed what led their becoming. It was the heart that made the years what they were—the heart in its finite capacity made infinite by the dwelling of the Lord. For though at nineteen-years-old I learned my dreams were possible, I didn't yet realize how small they were. The Lord outdid me. He continually showed me a better way.

I do not know what will be in the coming years, my older self with such knowledge will smile at such ignorance, but I do know He will be in them all, in every raindrop and frost, in every darkness, bearing great light. I am at the mercy of the Lord both in what I have done or how I have failed and in what will be done. In his hands, I am safe and constantly draw nearer towards my end to beget a new beginning.

"And if he is afraid that every cloud will bring rain, he will never harvest his crops. You don't know where the wind will blow...But you can't understand what he's doing. Begin planting early in the morning and don't stop working until evening. This is because you don't know which things you do will succeed. It is even possible that everything you do will succeed" (Ecclesiastes 11:4-6)

Claire Leiter is located out of Minneapolis, MN.
For media inquiries, please visit www.claireleiter.com.

Made in the USA
Middletown, DE
02 February 2017